# ON THE GREAT REUNION INGATHERING JOURNEY

## A STUDY FOR THE JOURNEY

SUSAN E. CRAIG

WESTBOW
PRESS®
A DIVISION OF THOMAS NELSON
& ZONDERVAN

WestBow Press books may be ordered through booksellers or by contacting:

WestBow Press
A Division of Thomas Nelson & Zondervan
1663 Liberty Drive
Bloomington, IN 47403
www.westbowpress.com
1 (866) 928-1240

ISBN: 978-1-5127-4023-3 (sc)
ISBN: 978-1-5127-4025-7 (hc)
ISBN: 978-1-5127-4024-0 (e)

Library of Congress Control Number: 2016906989

Print information available on the last page.

WestBow Press rev. date: 4/28/2016

# CONTENTS

# ABOUT THE AUTHOR

I grew up in New Jersey and left to attend college in Syracuse, New York. During college I took the opportunity to study a year in Greece. After college I entered the US Navy and served for fifteen years, being stationed in places such as Japan, Italy and Turkey. Now widowed with one son and living in Ohio.

I have found that I rarely follow the usual route in many things. My journey of faith did not follow the common paths that we hear most often. I grew up in a family that felt organized religious expression many times created unnecessary blocks in life that were not good and often times were discriminatory. So we, as a family, avoided church going as a rule.

However there was something that piqued my curiosity enough for me to investigate the origin of things on my own. Having a science background, I became curious to explore how the world came to be and what it that informed the order that was evident throughout nature. From the smallest things to the vastness of the universe, there is an order that defies the probability of random chance. My loves of reading and history set me on a journey of questioning and searching the cycles that seemed to be prevalent in civilizations. What caused most to rise and fall then in some cases to disappear from history. There was one that seemed to defy this pattern. The history book that told of this group also mentioned several others that many thought as fictional until later archeology found them. I explored as many avenues as I possibly could to explain patterns and the origins.

When I could no longer argue that there was not an overarching intelligence at work in the universe, I started looking into the various expressions of belief in this intelligence that exist. I explored many options atheist, agnostic, animist, and several differing theistic belief systems. I was looking for a consistency through the ages and coherency of message throughout. I even looked at the possibility that this intelligence could and would communicate with His creation in whatever means that individual or group could best fathom. Having come to a profound belief in the God of the Bible, I am now on a continuing journey of exploration for understanding.

This book is part of my continuing study into the love and provision that God continues to shower on this world. I feel that the Old Testament is foundational and informs the teachings found in the Gospel of the New Testament. As such, an understanding of this foundation can and does deepen our understanding for our journey with God and to God's home for us.

*"By day the Lord directs his love,*
*At night his song is with me*
*A prayer to the God of my life."*
*Psalms 42: 8*

# ACKNOWLEDGEMENTS

I would like to thank the pastoral staff and teachers at my home church, Stanwood Community, who patiently endured my questions about Biblical texts. Graciously and generously giving of their time. Without this help, advice, and encouragement I would have hesitated to put forward this book.

Dr. Steve Moroney, Head of the Department of Theology at Malone University, was invaluable in encouraging me towards deeper understanding Biblical interpretation. I would like to thank him for taking time out of his busy schedule to read over this work and offer suggestions.

Lastly and most importantly, God who continues to encourage and guide my curiosity to study and to investigate His Word. He continues to lead me to new depths within His living Word that had previously been confusing and illuminated them with a new understanding. For He has promised and I have confidence in His promise.

*"But the Advocate, the Holy Spirit,*
*Whom the Father will send in my name,*
*Will teach you all things*
*And will remind you of everything*
*I have said to you."*
*John 14: 26*

# FOREWORD

The Old Testament, or Hebrew Scriptures, constitute approximately three-fourths of the Christian Bible. Yet many Christians rarely read from the Old Testament, except occasional ventures into selected books such as Genesis, Psalms, and Proverbs. Have you ever been puzzled over how the Old Testament relates to the New Testament to form a unified Bible? Sue Craig's book may be just what you need to make better sense of it all.

The introduction clearly signals the direction of her study. God wants to commune with his people and though we have sinfully strayed from his instructions, God continually pursues us—from Noah to Abraham to Moses and the Tabernacle constructed under his leadership. Craig relates the Old Testament themes of private communion with God (the feast of booths) and being led by God (the moving cloud/pillar and anointing with oil) to the New Testament themes of private prayer and being led by the Spirit who indwells God's people. From the very beginning we see God's purpose of "tabernacling" with his people and enjoying an intimate relationship with them, dwelling eternally with his people in the new heaven and new earth.

In the body of the work Craig traces the unfolding of God's covenants, which invite us to be reconciled and restored to close relation with him. She summarizes

God's word spoken through his prophets, foretelling of the coming Messiah. Craig manages, as well, to touch on the laws and customs that God used to show his people what righteousness and holiness look like, and to show us just how far we fall short of that standard on our own. The book offers an in-depth study of the Old Testament tabernacle and the New Testament tabernacle/temple by which God lives in and among his people, all of whom serve as priests, follow an annual calendar, and observe practices that mirror those under the old covenant. Craig's book helps us look both backward and forward, and helps us grasp both the theological/intellectual as well as the practical/ devotional aspects of Scripture. In the vein of other recent biblical theologies that assist us in connecting the Old and New Testaments, this study is full of insights for inquisitive readers.

Stephen K. Moroney, Ph.D.
Professor of Theology, Malone University

# PRELUDE

## "Come Tabernacle with God"

## Psalm -122 - A song of ascent (NIV)

*I rejoiced with those who said to me,*
*"Let us go to the house of the LORD."*

*Our feet are standing in your gates Jerusalem.*

*Jerusalem is built like a city that is closely compacted together.*
*That is where the tribes go up*

*— The tribes of the LORD —*
*To praise the name of the LORD*

*According to the statute given to Israel.*
*There stand the thrones for judgement,*
*The thrones of the house of David.*

*Pray for the peace of Jerusalem:*
*"May those who love you be secure.*
*May there be peace within your walls*
*And security within your citadels."*

*For the sake of my family and friends,*
*I will say, "Peace be within you."*
*For the sake of the house of the LORD our God*
*I will seek your prosperity*

# PREFACE

This study started out as a look into what was God's design and purpose for the Old Testament Tabernacle as it relates to our Temple where the Holy Spirit comes to tabernacle with Christ's disciples. This first Tabernacle was the place God instructed Moses to construct from the pattern that is in heaven. This first Tabernacle was to be constructed so as to be a fitting place for God to come and meet with the Israelites. It was the specified place where they could come to seek God and where God's forgiveness and instruction could be obtained. Thus, could it inform us about how we were to prepare and care for the place where we invite God the Holy Spirit to come and live within us?

It, the study, became much more as it went along. For as I looked at the reason God established the Tabernacle, I had to look at the meaning of Covenant as established by God. This then led to looking at God's faithful and persistent announcements and offers of the opportunities of restoration of our union with God. So in the end this has become a look at the many times God has promised to gather in a harvest of His people and then what He has told us of how we should prepare for this ingathering.

This study has led me to a deep appreciation and wonder at God's faithful fulfillment of the covenant requirement to make all effort to restore the covenant breaker to good standing and compliance within the covenant conditions.

# INTRODUCTION

Since the time of creation, God has always had the desire for a personal and supremely intimate relationship with the creation that He had made in His image [man]. When this relationship was broken by a failure to fulfill assigned duties and evasion of responsibility, man was permitted to go his own way. Since then God has made several offerings of the opportunity of return. His desire seeking to reestablish this relationship has endured throughout time. During these times of offering, God has provided shelters (Tabernacles) where man could come and meet with Him. These were at other times called booths or arks. One definition of the word booth is a small private space. Today this is similar in meaning to the closet that Christ advised us to repair to when we wished to have converse with God. Over time as God has repeatedly brought His chosen people to the place He had promised to prepare for His own. He gave those who would make the return, guidelines for the journey. So this is an examination of the various times that God has gathered His people. Looking these in gatherings to learn lessons for the journey He has called us to join at this time.

At the time of Creation, all the people were aware of God's standards. These standards were set in place by God so that we could maintain this especially close loving relationship with our maker. All men knew what was expected and what was acceptable for worshiping God. Each person, having the gift of free will, was to be responsible for his own contributions and actions. Each one walked and talked face to face with God freely in complete harmony. This personal, private and totally intimate relationship was later symbolically commemorated in the Hebrew Festival of Tabernacles. This festival is set in the calendar at the completion of the yearly cycle symbolic of God's end desire. It was to be a celebration remembering God's provision, love and faithfulness. The festival and attendant feast memorializing the many times of His faithfully fulfilled promises. One of these was the remembrance of the time of the fulfillment of His promise to Abraham that He would gather His people into the land He had prepared for them[1]. This annual feast stands as a reminder of God's willingness to walk with, provide for, and guide us along our journey. During Tabernacles each celebrant was to construct his own place for withdrawing to be privately with God. It is thus a reminder of the promise He has given to the world to again gather His people into the home He has prepared for them.

During this Festival time each person was to retreat into a personally constructed space to reside with God. This structure was to be set apart from the day to day life. Yet not totally separated from it. This most often was achieved by being constructed external to the home yet not detached from it. Frequently this special structure was built upon the roofs of their homes.

This structure could be considered a picture of the tabernacle we are to have today under the New Covenant. One of the words used to translate the Hebrew word is dwelling. This place is where we are able to retire for our

---

[1] Moses (Genesis 12: 7 and Genesis 15: 14). 1973. *Holy Bible*. Grand Rapids, Michigan: Zondervan. Accessed 2015 (Holy Bible 1973)

private time with God and to dwell/communicate with Him. That place within the tent of our body which God has filled with the Holy Spirit. Thus this place, in addition to being commemorative of the time God gathered the children of Israel into the land He has reserved for them; it can be, also, again a place where the Shekinah of God makes its presence known. It is a reminder of our hope and joy at the promises He has given. That is the promise to, again, gather His people to Him in a personal relationship in the home He is preparing for us.

God's plan for this journey of our return, began even as Adam and Eve paid the consequence of their disobedience. This consequence was not only expulsion from Eden but also the severing of their daily intimate relationship. Nonetheless, men continued to be aware of the proper ways that God had established for communication and association with Him after expulsion from community with God [Eden]. Some men chose to abide by these requirements, while others, for reasons of their own chose to short on some of these standards. Then, when their offering was rejected for not meeting God's requirements, they became resentful. We have the example of Cain and Abel that gives an instance of the extreme results of the choices each freely made. Abel and Cain both knew the parameters for making an acceptable offerings to God. Abel chose to adhere to those parameters while Cain chose to short God in his offering. Cain then lashed out in jealousy and anger that his, Cain's, offering was considered insufficient. Down through history some have continued to lash out, some have departed in anger to set up systems that satisfied their own feelings and desires, and always there were some who repented and corrected their ways. In this time we have been given an opportunity to choose to take steps towards reestablishing this intimate relationship. These opportunities came to us not because we've earned them but because it was God's desire and purpose for us to have the opportunity choose to return of our own free will.

> *"He has saved us and called us to a holy life — not because of anything we have done but because of his own purpose and grace. This grace was given us in Christ Jesus before the beginning of time."*
> *[2 Timothy 1:9]*

As the distance from the expulsion from Eden grew, the more incomplete or corrupted the instructions became as the customs and practices of the parents and community groups were passed on to succeeding generations. Each practicing as they understood what had been passed down to them and/or cherry-picking the ones that they ones they liked to follow and ignoring those which they didn't. Schisms occurred within each group as the same issues that caused the original rift in our relationship with God continued to arise; disobedience, shifting responsibility, lying for personal benefit, greed, hunger for power, and resentment. In a phrase that is found at times in the Bible just prior to the God's chosen people going astray;

> *"In those days they had no king; everyone did as they saw fit."* *[Judges 21: 25].*

They, the peoples before the establishment of Israel, might have had temporal kings but rarely was the one true King's sovereignty given the recognition due to Him. Man continued to not seek the guidance and instruction of his Maker but went with what in each individual's understanding seemed right picking and choosing what pleased themselves.

In time, God desiring reconciliation with His creation, chose a people to be his ambassadors and examples for what God had established as right, good and proper. This set of standards were the guidelines for our ability to approach Him with confidence and love; not in fear. They are, also, instructions for how we should be dealing with each other so as to demonstrate to the world the benefits found in abiding in God's instruction and Word.

For this purpose Noah was selected first to call people back to God. Then to provide a safe shelter to God's creatures who chose to return to a relationship with Him when He would cleanse the earth of the pollution to His creation caused by sin. This meant that the people would have to voluntarily accept the proffered safety. This was a challenge for the earth had never before had even experienced a rain storm before. So what Noah was warning about was something which was outside of the experience of mankind prior to the Flood.

This invitation to the world was for their return to God, His ways and communion. The acceptance of His invitation signaled a belief in His word by then entering into the first Covenant Ark to escape a coming flood. Man had never experienced rain so a flood was beyond his comprehension and would have to be accepted on faith. After the flood, God again set man on a clean world, He gave us the promise that through a descendant of Noah's son Shem that He would provide another sheltering for the world. It would be offered to those of the world who were willing to receive and accept the offer. It was Shem's descendant, Abraham, who God chose. He was given instructions that if we could perfectly adhere to would gain our access to God. When perfectly followed they were to provide the perfect example of community designed by God to call peoples of the world back to Him. Then through the ages Abraham's descendant

David's line would produce for us the Savior who brought us the offering of Grace should we again choose to enter into its shelter.

A major step in the implementation of God's design for reestablishing the path for the restoration of our relationship with Him was the establishment of Israel. This entailed creating a visible people group who were to be called by His name. In some circles the meaning of this name carries implications of God's striving perseverance and His governing sovereignty.[2] At this time God gave us a visible place of meeting where man could go to meet with Him, a written record of the requirements and standards of behavior for gaining access to God's presence as well as being His representatives before the world. For the safety of the people, He appointed from among the nation, a tribe to be suitable intermediaries and intercessors. This protection was for all who would fall short of the requirements for safe entrance before God. This place where the people could meet with God was the Tabernacle and the appointed tribe was the tribe of Levi.

The Tabernacle was given to the community and just as Noah was given specific instructions for the construction of the ark, Israel was given specific instructions for the construction, the necessary appointments for it, the maintenance that was to be performed, and the preparations for serving before God in this place. The Tabernacle was to travel with His people on their daily journey to the home God had established for them. Reassuring them of God's guidance, provision and protection along their journey. It served as a visible sign and reminder that God was with them and what was expected of them as His people. During this period the container [the Ark of the

---

[2] 2000 - 2014. *Abarim Publications: sources.* http://www.abarim-publications.com/Meaning/Israel.html#.VVaRIPlViko

Covenant] holding the instructions for proper living led the way following God's glory.

As they entered into the Promised Land, God instructed them to commemorate this period when they lived in tents and traveled with Him as he gathered them in from the far place. He instructed them to celebrate this time with a feast. During this feast they were to construct booths in which to withdraw to have private time with God on a one to one basis.

Then as they settled into the land that was given to them they centralized the location of the Tabernacle and created a 'permanent' structure, temple, to house a ceremonial meeting place with God. While this was to honor God's stability and permanence it also unfortunately removed God from being within sight during the day to day living of life. Yet annually each family during the Feast days would construct booths to which they would repair during this holy days celebration.

Later on the New Covenant established a royal priesthood under Christ's High Priesthood with a temple which is our body. Once again God can and will travel with us in our daily travels if we again choose to have this intimate a relationship with Him. As at the time of Moses, when God selected a people to be called by His name, now under the New Covenant we are a new people who are called by His name. Once again we are instructed to designate a 'closet' to which we can go for private conversation with our God and Savior.

> "But thou, when thou prayest, enter into thy closet, and when thou hast shut thy door, pray to thy Father which is in secret; and thy Father which seeth in secret shall reward thee openly."
> [Matthew 6: 6 KJV]

While the Israelites were on their journey, they were not to move unless God did. Similarly those chosen to serve before God in the Temple were to receive an anointing before commencing their temple service. This anointing, done by the pouring out of a holy oil over them, was a symbolic of an anointing with the Holy Spirit. Thus when the new priesthood was initiated, those who followed and walked with Christ, were to wait to receive an anointing. Just as before, Christ told his Apostles to wait, before going out on the Great Commission for the Holy Spirit to come and not only be with them but in them.

> *"On one occasion, while he was eating with them, he gave them this command: "Do not leave Jerusalem, but wait for the gift my Father promised, which you have heard me speak about. For John baptized with, water but in a few days you will be baptized with the Holy Spirit." [Acts 1: 4, 5].*

We should, also, ensure that we have waited upon God in all our efforts to continue the Great Commission; and in our services to God. In order to better render this worship it behooves us to maintain the place where God has come to Tabernacle with us.

This is a study of what God has told us about our Tabernacle. Looking first at what was lost and the results of that loss that led to God instituting this instructive festival. Then considering God's plan for reestablishing the intimate relationship entailed in tabernacling (or dwelling) with God. Then looking at the Festival of Tabernacles and its place in the order of calendar of celebrations that God instituted. Finally studying what was His direction for the proper structuring and accoutrements for our tabernacles.

He has even given us guidelines to maintain and guard it so we can enjoy a continual close loving intimate relationship with our Maker. For just as the Apostles were not to go out to the world without the indwelling of the Holy Spirit, so today we should seek the guiding of the Holy Spirit before we go out into our world.

It seemed proper to look at what might have been our relationship as it was enjoyed in the beginning that God was desirous of restoring. This gives a better picture of what God is calling us to return to in relationship. We then can exercise our God given free-will to choose for ourselves to desire the return.

Then the causes and consequences of man's actions that lead to the separation necessitating a plan for restoration. Discovering that the plan of restoration and return as God would lay it out for us, was in God's plan even before our separation from Him. Considering what we learned via the Covenants, Prophets and His Commandments and Laws we are given a very detailed exposition of what was lost, what was required, and what would be offered. This lead to noticing the pattern of steps in His plan that were commemorated, to be watched for, and celebrated in the teaching tools that were part of the God ordained Tabernacle and later Temple yearly cycle of worship. Finally considering what were God's directions for the proper set up and functioning of the Tabernacle and Temple.

Then seeing if these directions could tell us something of how these things work under the New Covenant. Especially in regard to the space within each of us where the Holy Spirit again interacts directly with the believers. The Apostles Peter and Paul variously called our bodies, tents and temples where we repair to communicate with our Lord. For again we are on a journey of ingathering towards the home that God has prepared for us. Because

God has called us out of bondage and paid the price for our freedom. We are on the journey, looking forward to God calling us home with the establishment of the New Jerusalem, New Earth and Heaven. As when God called Israel out of Egypt to a citizenship in their Promised Land, we are being prepared for entry as citizens into our home that is being prepared for us.

> *"But our citizenship is in heaven. And we eagerly await a Savior from there, the Lord Jesus Christ, who, by the power that enables him to bring everything under his control, will transform our lowly bodies so that they will be like his glorious body." [Philippians 3: 20, 21]*

So we as can be said to again be on a journey of ingathering with God to the place He has prepared for us the events and instructions from the previous ingathering can help us on our current journey. Now as then when He brought Israel out from Egypt, He has made possible our freedom from slavery. Then He led them away from this bondage and into their Promised Land. Now again He has opened the doors that hold man in bondage. He has again offered freedom to people from the bondage to sin and trespass debt. Now begins our journey home to Him. As then, now again we have the promise that He will guide and protect us on the way. During that journey we are promised, again, that He will be with us along the way.

For God has promised to bring His remnant into His house many times and in many ways. One of those times was as He brought the nation of Israel into the Promised Land.

*"When you and your children return to the Lord your God and obey him with all your heart and with all your soul according to everything I command you today, then the Lord your God will restore your fortunes and have compassion on you and gather you again from all the nations where he scattered you. Even if you have been banished to the most distant land under the heavens, from there the Lord your God will gather you and bring you back." [Deuteronomy 30: 2-5]*

Then the promise is again restated at the initiation of a New Covenant. This New Covenant brought to the whole world the Good News of Salvation, also reconfirmed God's promise to gather His people into His house.

*"And he will send his angels with a loud trumpet call, and they will gather his elect from the four winds, from one end of the heavens to the other." [Matthew 34: 31]*

So let us look at what those of history were told about God's desire for a restored the relationship between Himself and His creation. Striving to know His instructions about how this restoration would come about. Then follow the proper construction, maintenance and serving within the shelter He desires for us. This being our Tent of Meeting where His people can repair to receive of His love, guidance and justice. This can inform us in our daily travels, for we are again on a journey to a promised home.

# CHAPTER 1

### ⟿

## Community of God at Creation

We are told that at the time of creation; there was no sorrow and there was no dying for the entirety of creation had been pronounced 'good' in His sight. This pronouncement was made the Lord God of Creation, who is by definition the Lord God of all holiness, goodness, righteousness, provision and judgement. It was into this environment that God placed the one creation made in His image. This environment was to be the created home especially designed and furnished for this creation [man]. It was God's intention that in this environment, man and God would have a continuous joyful loving association and fellowship. This fellowship was totally free, intimate, and without shame for nothing was held back or hidden from any party within this relationship. Shame is the desire to keep another from knowing or seeing something that is within us or we have done.

This is environment of joy, peace and intimacy is what all creation yearns to return to. For all creation, not just mankind, has been caught up in the consequences of man's choices. For unfortunately the consequences of our actions affect more than our self and this was the first devastating example of this truth. Thus as God does not fail nor go back on his word, we have some indications what the New Earth will be like when creation is resurrected along with redeemed mankind and again God will abide daily with His creation.

God is holy and pure and nothing that is not both pure and holy or has accepted the offered perfect covering can be permitted to survive in His presence. What is it to be holy? Holy is the state of having no darkness or impurity within or anywhere surrounding one. Nor can there be any accepting of anything that does not come up to these standards into the holy one's presence without destroying that state. It is a perfection of presence, person, probity and proximity. This is why when man allowed darkness into his being a separation would need to occur. Unfortunately this separation applied to all creation not just erring man. Thus when man fell short he had to depart for anything that did not come up to the standard of holiness could not be in God's presence and survive. For anything impure to be allowed to enter either the holiness is destroyed or that pollution is destroyed to maintain the holiness. Any such impurities if allowed weaken would diminish the ideal and destroy the perfection. This is the first time God refrained from destroying His creation.

One of the gifts from God that was designed to make him [man] in God's image is thought to be the gift of free will. So man was given free will of choice within the structure that had been specifically made for his benefit and as a proper setting for the intimate connection with his Creator. This means that responsibility for, and the consequences of those choices were on their shoulders. Just as Adam's and Eve's choices carried consequences for them, it carries down to us through the ages. Just as their choices affected the world we live in today, so it is that this story instructs us that our choices will have an effect on those around us. Thus we not only bear the results of our choices; we bear the burden of how our actions affect those who are around us as well. We have been given the guidelines that are the better path but it is our choice to follow or try something that in our mind attracts us or seems logical. Many times what seems logical to our thinking is not so in God's for His thought patterns are beyond ours;

> *"For my thoughts are not your thoughts, neither are your ways my ways," declares the Lord. "As the heavens are higher than the earth, so are my ways higher than your ways and my thoughts than your thoughts." [Isaiah 55: 8, 9]*

In saying that not only are His thought processes not like ours, He is in addition saying that His ways and standards are superior to those of our own devising.

One of our [man's] besetting characteristics to this day, is a desire to evade the negative consequences of our errors and our sense of fairness wishes to deny the fact that our actions do not only redound to us but also affect those around us. In addition we will go to great lengths to protect those we care for from the discomforts that come when they make bad choices.

Between man and God there had been a totally intimate open sharing in honesty and respect. When man acted on his questioning and his doubting of the truthfulness and goodness of God this caused a breach in the relationship. By acting on that doubt man discovered good and evil. God being thoroughly truthful and just had to allow the promised consequences to go forward with death coming into being for the disobedience. The consequence was promised when man was told not eat to of the trees at the

center of Eden. This created a wall within man's being where
he did not wish God to see and destroyed the openness and
joy of association that had existed. God did not put up this
wall man did.

Man's original purpose in Eden was not merely as
caretaker and cultivator of the garden but it could be said
to have, also, been as priestly guardian of the sacred and
holy precincts of the garden. Thus the garden in this sense
was the original temple of God, making the later structures
of the Tabernacle and the Temple were mere reflections of
what was and what will be the New Jerusalem at the time
of the great reunion and restoration. This is indicated in the
choice of words God records in Genesis. These words are
the same as those that are used later in describing priestly
purpose while serving the Tabernacle and later Temples.[3]
In Genesis 2: 15 it says:

> And the Lord God took the man and put him in
> the Garden of Eden to tend and guard and keep
> it. [AMPC]

The Hebrew words translated as tend and guard and
keep were the ones later used in Numbers to describe the
work of the priests serving the Tabernacle and Temple. So
not only was man functioning as groundskeeper, he was to
protect and serve the place of communion with God. The
passage that uses these words in the description of priestly
duties reads;

> And they shall keep all the instruments and
> furnishings of the Tent of Meeting and take

---

[3] Beale, G. K. 2004. *The Temple and the Church's Mission; a biblical theology
of the dwelling place of God.* Downers Grove, Illinois: Intervarsity Press

*charge of [attending] the Israelites, to serve in the
tabernacle. [Numbers 3: 8 AMPC]*

This, also, foreshadows the priestly duties of the New
Covenant Royal Priesthood in the restored creation. Thus
in Adam's transgression not only was there a defiance of
God's instruction there was the failure in duty of guarding
the precinct of God's sanctuary.

There is indication that governance was also within the
job description as dominion is a term of governance. At
Creation's completion Adam was given rule over it. There
is the implication of expanding influence outward from the
precincts of the immediate garden. There are scriptures
that indicate that with the desired restoration, and man's
reconciliation with God brings a restoration of both the
priestly and ruling privileges that were lost in addition to
the intimate and personal interaction. For in Revelation they
sing a new song:

> *And they sang a new song, saying: "You are
> worthy to take the scroll and to open its seals,
> because you were slain, and with your blood you
> purchased for God persons from every tribe and
> language and people and nation. You have made
> them to be a kingdom and priests to serve our God,
> and they will reign on the earth." [Revelation 5:
> 9, 10]*

# CHAPTER 2

## The Separation

Once this wall went up, God had to withdraw His personal connection from within mankind. This separation left a void within the soul of man. It is this void that man has been trying to fill in any way and by any means possible ever since our departure from Eden was enforced and sealed. This void has created a restlessness that impels man to a continual searching for a completion of himself that would alleviate the aching this hole left. As each of us was designed to have a place to meet with God; the inner emptiness is similar to the picture of the emptiness of the Tabernacle and later the Temple when God withdrew his presence. For the Temple/Tabernacle were visible and a physical representation of a place for man to repair to God. Thus it was the equivalent of the inner void that is within each of us created when God withdrew. Until the Inner Court of our Tabernacle is again filled with the glory of God there will continue to be a restless sense of incompleteness within our being.

Man chose to doubt God's word. In the moment man decided to test God's word that death would come if they ate fruit from one of the trees at the center of Eden, man was expressing doubt in God's veracity and that He would truly follow through on His word. In allowing darkness of temptation access to the Garden, Adam and Eve slacked on their responsibilities of guarding and tending it and so disobeyed God's instruction and delegation of purpose.

God then gave man multiple chances to repent and return. It was a three step event, God gave man multiple chances. With that first bite a recognition of the error came flooding in and along with it a sense of shame. Shame is the inner prompting to hide or cover over our actions. Adam and Eve had both of these reactions, they hid and made efforts to cover themselves. God asked them to tell Him what and why, but they refused to confess responsibility. If man had come clean would they have been expelled? I do not know but am inclined to say no for as the Prophet Jonah said;

> *"I knew that you are a gracious and compassionate*
> *God, slow to anger and abounding in love, a God*
> *who relents from sending calamity." [Jonah 4: 2]*

When questioned as to why they did the act, Adam and Eve, each tried shifting responsibility for their choice to another. Again it is never said straight out, God gave them a couple of chances to own up to their actions and doubting; perhaps if they had asked forgiveness, grace would have been applied at that time. But like many of us when confronted with the results of our ill-advised actions they continued to try to shift the responsibility to others.

As with any intimate relationship when it is violated a consequence would have to take place. For without acknowledgement of error a withdrawal will take place. Before any repair of this breach can be accomplished a recognition and acknowledgement of the error is the minimum repentance for a reconciliation or restoration to occur. When genuine love and affection are wronged, the wronged one will do the sinner the greatest service by allowing them to experience the results of the choice they made rather than shielding them from the pain.

In God's righteousness and justice He allowed the stated consequences to go forward all the time setting in motion the plan for a return to the relationship. In the case of man the consequences entailed physical and emotional separation from his Maker, loss of the peace, joy and loving association in Eden, struggle and pain in sustaining himself, and in the end death. Separation – Not only was the close connection with God broken but banishment from his daily presence and physical expulsion from Eden. Loss – Other than the loss of the perfection of Eden, the close loving fellowship was shattered and there was a withdrawal of the part within each that facilitated the connection to God. Struggle and pain – while work was done in tending to Eden now this effort would entail meeting with resistance, discomfort, and obstacles. Death – while death was not immediate it did come. Just as the after effects of some of our foolish choices do not have immediate presentation but come several years later, death came to mankind. Until we reach a full appreciation of the loss we cannot truly make the needed turning from the thoughts, attitudes and actions that led us away.

This then is the origin of the aching restlessness at the core of mankind as down through the ages humans have sought in endless ways to assuage the longing hunger. Among the means that have been tried are spiritual (worshiping the created not the Creator to the fantastic), pharmaceutical (either as pain relief or hallucinogenic), academic (from philosophic, and science to ideological), relational (idolization or consuming) and the means that is thought of most often, materially (by worshiping things or acquisitiveness). Anything that turns our focus away from God for extended lengths of time is seriously capable of becoming an idol with which we try to fill the God shaped hole in our lives.

As He did in Eden, God has repeatedly placed before us His conditions for restoring our relationship. In His omniscience He knew our comprehension and acceptance would be gradual. That this would happen when and only when we recognized our inability to accomplish these requirements with our abilities would we be ready to seek the help needed to be able to safely come into His holy presence. So it was that revelation of His plan came over time. Then as mankind came to the conclusion that in fact help, forgiveness and covering were needed before they could to be restored to a wholeness, God placed His Grace before mankind for man to choose freely.

# CHAPTER 3

⁓

## The plan of salvation

The plan of salvation is God's way of setting out a course by which man can again come to dwell in His tents. It is the means by which we can again enter His presence in joy and confidence. It is our guide and initial step towards the reconciliation that all creation longs for.

As God is not taken by surprise with anything that occurs, He knew that His creature would fumble and drop the ball when learning to use responsibly the gift of freedom. Therefore God had the plan by which there would be an opportunity for a reconciliation and restoration of the relationship with mankind all ready to go. These were plans that would be made by gradual revelation. These revelations were intended to bring man to an awareness of the loss, the requirements and standards needed to again enter into God's presence and his need for forgiveness. Once a desire for what was lost is gained man seeks a restoration. Part of this desire seeks to understand the conditions to be met. This brings a comprehension of his inability to meet these standards by his own efforts. Creating a realization of his need for forgiveness. Then God would make available to those who would freely choose it, the gift of grace. Throughout this journey through time reassurances were given that there would be one who would come with this gift only when man had full knowledge that in his own strength and fallen state he was incapable of perfectly abiding in the requirements of righteousness.

This process needed four things for completion. First off it needed some means of making a complete and full payment for the transgressions that held us in slavery to the world. Then an offer of debt forgiveness needs to be made to those held in bondage by worldly blandishments. This forgiveness then must be accepted by those who had committed punishable offenses against the holiness of God. Once the Grace of freedom and pardon has been freely acknowledged as needed and accepted. Then a reconciliation journey starts us on the road which will bring us again into unity with God in His fullness. Lastly, there will come the restoration when again we will see Him again face to face.

God's intention to offer mankind this opportunity was there from the beginning. Even before the establishment of the Hebrew nation, a picture of the coming salvation was given in the story of Noah, a man who walked before God. In this story, we have one who calls people to return to a right regard for God. Noah made this call to any and all willing to listen and respond. Then the offer is made for all who wished to voluntarily enter into a protective shelter from a coming storm. Then after the storm had passed they were brought to a world made clean.

Well before being instructed to build the Ark, Noah was walking with God and calling people to make a return to God. Then as the rains started to fall he continued to call to the people to accept God and His offer of protection. The doors only closed at God's command. Then the storm

11

came and washed the world clean of all that had rejected God. In the end the Ark came to rest on a newly cleansed world into which Noah and all with him were sent out to prosper and grow. Picturing in compressed time the call of Jesus to all people to a return to a right standing with and a proper understanding of God, then the coming storm of tribulation, finally being brought to a new heaven and earth in which to prosper.

Under God's plan from the beginning there would be a period where man would be given opportunity to see what was required of one who would enter into an intimate walk with God. During this time certain festivals and sacrifices were given as encouragements as we discovered how inadequate we can be in attempting the required perfection. This period was also supposed to be a time when God's people were to be an attractive example to the world showing the myriad advantages to living in God's way. The Law was given so we would know exactly what needed to be done perfectly to have any hope of having a personal walk with God. Instructions for daily life and customs were reminders of how we were to act so as to be examples of God before the world who does not recognize Him. The sacrifices were incomplete examples of the cost that would be required for the full payment needed to satisfy the debts we incur daily. The Festivals were given to be encouraging reminders and teaching tools of God's provision, desire, forgiveness, grace, and love. God in His wisdom gave us the intent for Christ's Advent in the purpose and function of the Tribe of Levi. This tribe was to stand as covering and intercessors for the people of the Nation of Israel, just as our Savior stands as our covering and intercessor before God.

Then the ultimate offer of forgiveness would be made available. First it was offered to the ones that had been chosen to represent God before the world and then to the entire world. It would be a total propitiation, restitution and atonement for all of mankind's debt to our Creator God. That means it was something that would make payments and actions sufficient for the satisfaction the entire load of debts and failures made by all mankind from all time. It would provide a covering for all the offences committed by every person to the loving God who graciously and abundantly provides for all. It would offer again the opportunity for us to begin again to tabernacle (live personally and daily with) God the Holy Spirit. This would cause the world to enter into what could possibly be called a betrothal period when the Son of God and those who have accepted the gift of His covering to prepare for the reunion that has been promised for the future.

During this period of betrothal the bride and groom both set about preparing themselves for the joyous time that is coming. In Jewish betrothal tradition there is a heightened sense of watchful anticipation on the part of the bride for she is not given any specific date or time for the bridegroom's return to fetch her. But she is expected to hold herself in alert readiness for the wedding feast that will occur at the time of His return and taking her to His home.

So an understanding of the path that God laid out for us is needed to best prepare us to be fitting brides. As we get to know deeply the desires and character of our beloved, the deeper our love, respect, and eager anticipation grows. Then it becomes a joy to strive to conform to those standards so that others will be able to see our partner in us. Just as when we say of a couple, "when you see one – you see the other"; so should we become.

Knowing what our beloved requires and expects helps us prepare for our new home. This new home is being prepared and will include all creation restored to the fullness of God's vision that he pronounced "very good" at the beginning. So a comprehension of what this new home will be like will help prepare us, with the Grace given to us, wish to enter in knowledgably and with great rejoicing.

# CHAPTER 4

## Incremental Revelation

From the start God's intention was that His plan was to be revealed incrementally. This was so that an awareness of the loss, the ideal, and the need would be inescapable and obvious. This is evident in how the complete plan was revealed. It was revealed over time and in bite sized chunks. The covenants given and made by God are an example of this. They build from a reminder of the unity, through choosing representatives for Him before the World, and the standards of Holiness that God requires of those who come before Him, then the offer of Grace. The Law was given so that we who like to think that we are in control of our own portions and wishing to have a relationship with God would understand what was required to be acceptable to enter into the presence of a Holy God and how utterly incapable we are of sustaining the needed perfection. This was necessary so that when the perfect gift would be offered we would know our absolute need of it. The prophets gave either indications of when the Redeemer would come, what He would bring to the world, where this would occur and what would the world's response would be; or they would prefigure the purposes of His coming.

Why was the complete plan of salvation not revealed in its sweeping beauty and totality all at one time? Could it be that God knows us so thoroughly that He knew that the way most of us need to come to a comprehension and an owning acceptance of the concepts encompassed in our salvation? That, that understanding could only be achieved in bite sized segments. Could this be an example of God knowing how his creation [man] best comes to understanding and owning for himself the outcome? Most of us need to see the reason and come to desire it before we can work diligently towards the goal set before us. Most of us have to truly want what we've come to understand as the desirability of the end goals for any sustained effort towards them. Then we have to come to an understanding of the conditions and requirements that were required to attain these goals. We, also, seem to like multiple chances to "get it right" on our own efforts. Human nature seems to have an inclination towards wishing to believe in our own self-sufficiency. We have to be convinced that we truly need help. Then and only when we recognize our inabilities, and are most of all willing give up our pride to ask for and accept the assistance and help we so desperately need to achieve these goals are we ready to proceed. When we finally reach this point of recognition and then accepting that gracious gift; only then were we ready to prepare our hearts and soul to be our personal tabernacle where we can go to commune and converse with God the Holy Spirit who would come to us upon acceptance of the gift of Grace made available by God the Son.

So it is that, God, while reassuring us throughout that a way for restoration would come, God allowed man to gradually understand his need. Secondly God let man come to see and understand all that was required to successfully reconcile and return to the presence of a supremely holy loved one. Then He placed before man the path to be freely chosen or rejected. So that now having recognized the need and accepting the Grace, we may enter into a relationship that works towards a full return. This process confirms that though God is omnipotent, He does not desire a relationship with man that is either coerced or forced. He rejoices in those relationships that are freely and willingly chosen.

God used the Covenants, Prophets, and the Commandments and Law to communicate His plan first to His people and thence to the world. The world was always included as evidenced that several times throughout this journey, God instructed His the chosen representatives (people), to remember and invite others to find shelter within a relationship to Him. At least five times God told those chosen to represent Him before the world that they were to reach out to other peoples of the world. First in the blessing given to Noah's sons [gentiles would find shelter in the tents of Shem]. Then Abraham was told that through one of his "seed" all nations would be blessed. The third time is found in the Law which makes provisions for the foreigners and sojourners in Israel. Then via the prophet Jonah who was given the mission to take God's word to some of the nastiest people then on the earth. Lastly it is found in the Great Commission give to us by the Lord Jesus the Christ.

As God's plan for reconciliation was being transmitted to the people chosen by Him and who chose to walk before Him, He continued to remind them that they were to share the knowledge of God with the world around them. They were and are today to be His ambassadors and exemplars of the glory that is God and the beauty of becoming all that He originally created us to be. We should keep this before us as it is that God's desire has not changed. As was illustrated in several of the parables told by Jesus, such as this one of the lost sheep.

> *"And if he finds it, truly I tell you, he is happier about that one sheep than about the ninety-nine that did not wander off. In the same way your Father in heaven is not willing that any of these little ones should perish." [Matthew 18: 13, 14]*

## I. Covenants [4]

Covenants – the covenant is a special kind of contract that holds all parties to a promise. A Biblical covenant has six parts: the parties to the agreement, the promises, the conditions, the duration, the sign, and the dedication. In the Bible the dedication was often sealed in blood as "in the blood there is life" [Leviticus 17:14]. There is also the knowledge and confidence in that God does not lie or go back on His Word, so that while man did, does and will fail to live up to his side of the covenants, God remains faithful to them. This fact has been recorded down through the ages. The covenants are designed to be advantageous to all parties involved. That being so, even when one party fails to live up to the terms, the other is expected to encourage the one that failed to return to good standing in the covenantal agreement. Thus it is that a covenant expects the faithful party to be longsuffering and to help the stumbling party to find ways to meet their side's obligations. This means that God has not and is not just waiting for us to mess up so as

---

[4] Benner, Jeff A. 2004. *The Holy Assembly and the Everlasting Covenant.* Accessed 2015. http://www.ancient-hebrew.org/holyassembly/chapter1.html.

to be released from His Word.[5] Most other civil contracts are not this, in that if one side breaches the terms of the contract, the contract is declared null and void and the remaining party is freed of any further obligation under the terms of that contract. As we have a covenantal relation with God, He still holds Himself to His given word even in the face of the many times man has failed to hold to his part of the contract. God has demonstrated His constancy to them as seen throughout history. And as seen throughout history He has made many offerings of a return to good standing to man. In the Bible there are six recorded covenants; Marriage, Noahic, Abrahamic, Mosaic, Davidic, and New.

In many places and instances contracts that were entered into by our forebears are binding on all the heirs and assigns. Most of us know who the heirs are; they are the direct descendants. Not all of us are conversant in what is meant by assigns. Well our current legal definition of this word is this; they are persons to whom property or an interest is transferred or may be transferred by conveyance, will, descent and distribution, or statute.[6] In this case we could say that assigns could be those who while they are not in the direct line of descent [genetic descendants of Abraham], but are those who have subscribed to the terms of the covenants and have been adopted. Under the Old Testament these would be gentiles who attached themselves to Israel by becoming proselytes. Now with the adoption we have received we are among the assigns to God's Word. We have confidence in this adoption for God has confirmed

---

[5] Hamilton, Jeffrey W. 2013. *The Importance of Covenants - Part II.* Accessed May 19, 2015. http://www.lavistachurchofchrist.org/LVSermons/ImportanceOfCovenants2.html.
[6] Farlex. 2015. *The Free Dictionary Legal.* Accessed May 16, 2015. http://legal-ictionary.thefreedictionary.com/assigns.

it in His covenants and spoken in His Word many times through the ages.

> *"For he chose us in him before the creation of the world to be holy and blameless in his sight. In love he predestined us for adoption to sonship through Jesus Christ, in accordance with his pleasure and will — to the praise of his glorious grace, which he has freely given us in the One he loves."*
> *[Ephesians 1: 4-6]*

So now all those who have accepted the Grace of God to become His children are inheritors of His blessings, chastisement, instruction and loving care.

## Marriage:

The first recorded covenant was the Marriage Covenant. This covenant is unique among the recorded covenants in that it was given to man to be entered into with his life partner (wife) with God as the confirming witness. The others are entered into between God and Man to forward the progress towards restoration. Originally given in Eden, perhaps it is also reassurance that God knew we would need to remember and have a reminder of what was going to be lost with our disobedience as it was given before that event. Thus Marriage was to be a reminding picture of the relationship that man had with God before the fall. It is structured to be a union that is jubilantly total and completely joyous. It was a union of two parts that would as a team make a whole. As such, it is this union that is so eagerly anticipated, expected, prepared for diligently, and will be utterly transforming. It has been shown that God has remained constant, faithful, forgiving, and true throughout the innumerable failures, breaches of contract, and false starts of the beloved, even to the point of leaving behind the glorious home in heaven to ensure that the beloved would be free to come to Him when the time of waiting (betrothal) would be completed.

Most of us think only of the covenant marriage in furtherance of the command to be fruitful and multiply. In that it established the structure of teamwork that has been proven the best for the protection and instruction of the succeeding generations. But it was intended as so much more. It was to be a picture of the give and take enjoyed by God in heaven and one that God wishes His creation (man) to participate in and enjoy too. It was to be a deep intermingling of mind, body and spirit. That is perhaps why the same word that is used in Genesis when the relationship between Adam and Eve is described is the same used when God describes in subsequent revelations the relationship He desires to have with His people.

> *"And Adam knew Eve his wife; and she conceived, and bare Cain, and said, I have gotten a man from the Lord." [Genesis 4: 1]*

It is this relationship of joyous openness that is without any hidden shame that has been offered to mankind. It is what we can anticipate as we start our journey of return.

The sign of this covenant is a ring or circle. There is contained in this sign the sense of totality, wholeness, original perfection, the self, the infinite, eternity, and timelessness. There is also the implication of cyclic motion and potential.

## Noahic:

The next covenant to be recorded is the Noahic. This covenant is given to all mankind as it was made before the establishment of the nation of Israel. Not only was the story a picture of the coming salvation but also this covenant was the first made between God and man. God has been faithful to it throughout history even in the face of many breaches of the contract by mankind. For it was not long after man had again been brought to a pristine world that he again started off in ways that seemed good in his own mind.

God gave the world as Covenant sign the rainbow. This stands as the sign of hope for all time that no matter the storms and tempest that God would sustain the world and things would eventually be better. This rainbow shines for us at the end of the storm when the sun again shines.

Within it we see a reconfirmation of the mandate of dominion that had been given in Eden. The entire covenant is found in Genesis 9: 1-17. We mostly focus on the promise to not destroy the earth with a flood again and the sign given that confirms the promise is still in force, the rainbow. It contained the assurance between man and God but covered all of the creatures of flesh that came with Noah on the ark in perpetuity that God would not destroy the earth again by flood waters. The injunction to be fruitful and multiply was reiterated to man and animal alike.

## Abrahamic:

This covenant was made with the man that God had chosen to become the father of the nation that was to become His representatives before the world. The covenant partner in this covenant with God was Abraham. Found in Genesis

17, it stipulates what God will do; make of a childless couple a great nation and that other nations would, also, come from his progeny. It contained the promise that from these descendants would come kings. One of these, though unstated, would become the King of kings. There is in this covenant the promise that from Abraham's descendants the entire world would obtain blessing. We now see that it was through this descendant, Jesus, how this blessing would come to all peoples of the world. It also established that He would plant His chosen people in a land of their own where previously they had been wanderers. Then it stipulates that Abraham and his descendants are to walk before God as his representatives and the sign of this covenant was individual and personal upon each descendant [circumcision].

The other fascinating thing about this covenant, was that Abraham was required to demonstrate his obedience and willing faith before the conditions would be put into force. This was an act that required Abraham to do something that seemed contradictory to instruction God had already given. This act seemed contrary to the injunction against killing another human-being and a destruction of the child of God's promise as well as asking to offer in sacrifice to God what was the dearest love of his heart. But by doing as God asked, prepare to offer Isaac as sacrifice to God, Abraham signaled his willing obedient submission to God. The implication being that God has blessings untold that awaits for the first willing step of obedient faith taken by His children before they can be given.

Circumcision was the sign given to affirm this covenant and was symbolic of being separated out as different to be God's special people. It was to be a constant physical reminder of being set apart from the rest of the world and being here for God's set purpose.

In sum, this covenant contains several conditions of interest to us. It reconfirmed God's intentions for the entire world in that there is contained in this covenant a statement concerning us (those not linked genealogically). It is the statement that the blessing of the world would come through Abraham. Not only was Abraham to have the Promised Land, and father many nations but it promised that through him the world would be blessed.

> *"Abraham will surely become a great and powerful nation, and all nations on earth will be blessed through him." [Genesis 18: 18]*

This covenant while made and signed by blood, was only truly in force after Abraham signified his complete obedience to walking before God. Showing that God sometimes requires us to step out in unquestioning faith in order to receive the fullness of His blessing.

In asking Abraham to sacrifice his beloved son of promise, God previewed the acts that must need be accomplished to achieve atonement. God would offer up His beloved Son as the sacrifice for the salvation of the world several centuries later. After this commitment there was an interval of 430 years before God would ingather His people into their promised home. A picture, as we now can surmise, of the interval between the crucifixion and offer of Grace to the coming of God's ingathering His people into the New Heaven and Earth home He is preparing for us.

## Mosaic:

This covenant contains within it all the standards of holiness and righteousness that need to be achieved and maintained perfectly and constantly for mankind to have a confident safe entry into God's presence. It is an exposition of the way to walk in righteousness before God. Adhering to these instructions is expected for one to be His exemplar before the world. If man would be solely in control of attaining or earning his right to return to an intimate daily relationship with God these are the basic requirements that God insists on. One must continuously and perfectly abide by each and every one of His commandments and laws to merit this access. As with all of the covenants there is a promise contained in it. This promise is that the Israelites would find prosperity by adhering to the conditions, and it says,

> *"Carefully follow the terms of this covenant, so that you may prosper in everything you do."* *[Deuteronomy 29: 9]*

The consequences are as plainly stated for to those who would falsely swear to this covenant,

> *"When such a person hears the words of this oath and they invoke a blessing on themselves, thinking, "I will be safe, even though I persist in going my own way," they will bring disaster on the watered land as well as the dry." [Deuteronomy 29: 19].*

It contains the sobering warning statement that one's actions will affect others around them. No matter that we think that our choices only the concern for one's self; it clearly indicates that others will always be impacted either directly or indirectly by our actions. These can either be immediate or somewhere down the road.

The symbols of this very comprehensive Covenant were the Ark of the Covenant and the Tablets of the Law. The Ark gives a reminder of the sheltering protection and salvation of the first ark constructed by Noah. Within it was placed symbols of the provision of God (manna), the sovereignty of God (Aaron's rod), and God's standard of holiness (the tablets of the law). The stone Tablets of the Law speak of the permanence and weight of God's standards and requirements for righteousness and holiness. The covering that was to be placed on this Ark, called the Mercy Seat, tells us of God's justice and mercy. On either side of the Ark were representations of the Cherubim the same heavenly creation that was set to guard the entrance to Eden after the expulsion of Adam and Eve. These seem to be in an attendant position rather than a guarding function.

In my estimation this covenant marked the mid-point in the revelation of God's plan of Salvation and Restoration. It gives us the conditions and requirements for return. It lets us make our own attempts to come up to the standards, ultimately showing us our insufficiency within our own abilities to meet them. It tells us the results and benefits that would follow should we continue in its guidelines as well as the consequences of failure. This was to make it abundantly clear why we would need a Redeemer capable of paying all of our debts. As the writer of Romans said;

> *"Now we know that whatever the law says, it says to those who are under the law, so that every mouth may be silenced and the whole world held accountable to God. Therefore no one will be declared righteous in God's sight by the works of the law; rather, through the law we become conscious of our sin." [Romans 3: 19, 20]*

## Davidic:

This covenant is more of an addendum to the previous two covenants. Why an addendum? Well it did not add new conditions or explanations but it confirmed to Israel that the Kinsman-Redeemer would come and out of which tribe He would come. It further narrowed it down to a specific family-line within that tribe. If there were any new conditions it would have arisen out of the question of why would one who would have priestly function not come out of the tribe chosen by God to serve before the Mercy Seat but from the tribe given the responsibility of civil governance? Under the Mosaic Covenant the tribe of Levi was set aside out of the nation of Israel to perform the necessary propitiation and atonement rituals for forgiveness for past errors and seeking grace in the coming year. Yet this covenant specifies that the Messiah would arise out of the Tribe of Judah. This tribe had been given the governance sovereignty over Israel. Signaling a return to the duality of purpose that was found in the beginning.

It strikes me that this is what caused much of the confusion that arose when Jesus began teaching and calling people to return to a proper relationship with God. The people of that time were looking for a political or military figure for that was the duties given to the descendants of Judah when a kingship was established. In the structure set up under the law only those of the tribe of Levi were permitted to perform priestly duties. Thus it was not expected that the Messiah coming from the tribe of Judah have jurisdiction over instruction in ways of a life of walking before God. Yet it signaled that God intended to again take both of these functions unto Himself in the End of Days and by delegation to those in His service.

The Davidic Covenant, was promised to King David at the time when King David expressed the desire of building a permanent structure for God's glory to reside in. He was deterred from building the Temple, but was told that one of his (David's) descendants would construct it [Solomon] and further that another of his descendants would come to Israel and be the ultimate King [Jesus]. In Second Samuel chapter seven the Lord declares to David through the prophet Samuel;

> *"When your days are over and you rest with your ancestors, I will raise up your offspring to succeed you, your own flesh and blood, and I will establish his kingdom. He is the one who will build a house for my Name, and I will establish the throne of his kingdom forever. I will be his father, and he will be my son. When he does wrong, I will punish him with a rod wielded by men, with floggings inflicted by human hands. But my love will never be taken away from him, as I took it away from Saul, whom I removed from before you. Your house and your kingdom will endure forever before me; your throne will be established forever." [Verses 12 through 16]*

Confirmation for this covenant could be seen as the fulfillment of several of the promises during David's lifetime and just shortly after his death. Those that happened during David's lifetime would be; that God would make David's name great, the borders of Israel were set, that Israel would have rest from war or attack. After his death two more came to fruition; David's line was established on the throne, and his son Solomon was permitted to construct the Temple in

Jerusalem and furnish it with the things that David had gathered specifically for it.[7]

## New:

This covenant is unique in that its contents would be revealed well prior to its establishment. It was prophesied by the prophet Jeremiah and recorded in Jeremiah 31: 31-40. This passage starts off with Jeremiah reporting;

> *"The days are coming," declares the Lord, "when I will make a new covenant."*

Thus Israel and by extension mankind could anticipate a new phase in our relationship with God. This was given several hundred years before the advent of Jesus Christ.

God declared that this Covenant would be unlike the previous ones that had been made with Israel.

> *"It will not be like the covenant I made with their ancestors when I took them by the hand to lead them out of Egypt, because they broke my covenant, though I was a husband to them,"* declares the Lord. [Jeremiah 31: 32]

For in this covenant is promised that the knowledge of God's law and desires would be written in the minds and hearts of believers and they would not need admonish their neighbors to know God as all will know Him. He promised that all would be forgiven and the sins would no longer be

---

[7] Grisanti, Michael A. 1999. *The Davidic Covenant*. 10 2. Accessed May 20, 2015. The Davidic Covenant TMS.pdf.

remembered. Then He stated that at time's conclusion His city would be reestablished to stand forever.

We, now, see that this covenant came into force with the crucifixion of Christ. At the time of prophesy, the sign for this Covenant was not established as one of the confirmations that the covenant was in effect was to seal it with blood. Nor was a continuing sign given. We now know this to be the communion table that signals a new community relationship and fellowship with God, it also is an affirmation of our new position as priests before God. This was because signs were normally given as the covenant was established and set in force. We can say that the sign of this covenant was the shedding of the Messiah's blood and the giving of His body in sacrificial atonement. We commemorate this every time we celebrate the taking of Communion. The act that sealed this covenant is the pouring out of the Holy Spirit into the hearts and souls of believers upon their acceptance of the Atonement made by Christ for their debts and trespasses and their acknowledging of His sovereignty.

## Conclusion

These covenants all are a stepped process towards restoring the communion and intimacy of the relationship that was broken so long ago. Each along the way perfectly setting up for man to be able to voluntarily choose to take the next step towards our reconciliation with God. For there is one thing that God gave us at the beginning and He has not violated; that is His gift of free will. It confirms that God will not force a relationship with Him because He desires our love and respect not our fear. Now we can confidently hope for the time when our Lord will tabernacle face to face with His people eternally. For now, it is that we are presented with the opportunity to have the Holy Spirit tabernacling within us comforting and counselling us should we attend to preparing and guarding our tabernacles.

The covenants give a picture of the depth of relationship that He would have with us. He has from the start desired to have complete and intimate knowing of each other to the point that if you see one you see the other. So that the character of God will be seen in the character of His people.

Contained in them we can surmise the sequencing of events established for our restoration. At the beginning there was a union that was breached. The repair of this needed first a recognition of what was lost and the perfection that was needed. Then there needed to be an expressed repentance and desire for forgiveness and restoration. Between the offering of this forgiveness and reunion there would be a period in which all would be preparing for the restoration. The culmination will be a renewal of our intimate relationship with God. We will have come full circle with the celebration of the "Marriage Feast of the Lamb".


## II. Prophets [8]

The prophets are another avenue God used to communicate the gradual revelation of His plan for a complete restoration with mankind. Down through the ages there have been men called to communicate a special word from God to the people these were called Prophets. Some were sent to admonish, others to warn, yet again some carried the reassurances of the coming Messiah. Of these latter some explained his mission and character,

---

[8] Henry, Matthew. n.d. *Matthew Henry Commentary on the Whole Bible, various prophets.*

others would point to time and location while others would prefigure why and what was coming. Part of our problems with understanding these prophesies comes from the fact that these revelations were recorded from the human perspective. This perspective sometimes leads to confusion, especially when an over-view of the completed restoration was given. When this kind of revelation was given it was difficult for man to discern the time span over which these events would take place.

The following prophets are but just a few of the references made within the Biblical texts that point to the Messiah. I in no ways can claim to have found them all.

## Hosea:

The Book of Hosea gives us a glimpse at both sides of the story of our relationship with God and our road to restoration. In Hosea, we see the lengths God is prepared to go to offer the grace of forgiveness to those He loves. It provides the example of the covenant requirement that the injured party make all efforts at restoring the other party to good standing. In Hosea's chosen bride Gomer, we see ourselves prone to wander in curiosity, prone to push away those who love us in our doubt of our worthiness, prone to going with the group not where our conscience says is correct. In God's economy the point to be driven home in this book is also contained the names of the main characters. Hosea[9] carries the meaning of salvation while the etymology of the name Gomer[10] points to the meanings

---

[9] 2000 - 2014. *Abarim Publications: sources* http://www.abarim-publications.com/Meaning/Hosea.html#.VaQIDvlViko

[10] 2000 - 2014. *Abarim Publications: sources* http://www.abarim-publications.com/Meaning/Gomer.html#.VaQKovlVikp

of perfect and complete. Thus these names mean in order point to Salvation, Perfect and Complete. When you add in Hosea's family name Beeri there is an additional layer of richness for it has several root meaning possibilities. Among these possibilities are a well of water, a covenant, providing and pure.[11] The primary understood definition being a well. So we have the names pointing us to a well providing a covenant of Salvation, perfect and complete.

The bride God instructed Hosea to take was one who was impure and came from less than illustrious family background. These were definitely not within the instructions that had been given to the Levites for the selection of their mates which were set in place for the purpose to maintain the perfection of presence, character and proximity surrounding a Holy God and those who were designated to serve at the altar. Hosea was of the tribe of Levi so when he would marry it was expected that he would follow the Law and guidelines for acceptable marriage partners; what God asked of Him were decidedly not within those instructions. After taking her as his bride, Hosea was instructed to forgive her again and again. Even to the point of traveling to a far land where she had given herself in slavery in order to purchase her redemption and freedom. After he had accomplished her redemption, he was then to receive her in his home again but only with her consent. Consider Gomer's dilemma, she knows what she has done, she has been deemed worthless by those around her, yet the one she most offended has given her freedom and asked her to return to him. Asked, can you imagine? He did not force or command, just asked and indicated she would be welcomed back should she choose to come home.

---

[11] 2000 - 2014. *Abarim Publications: sources* http://www.abarim-publications.com/Meaning/Beeri.html#Vj4EaLerRG8

In Eden we were part of a covenant union with God but we went astray. God is very up front with Hosea as to the reason behind his instructions for Hosea's marriage, it was to be an earthly picture of how Israel was treating their covenant with God.

> *"When the Lord began to speak through Hosea, the Lord said to him, "Go, marry a promiscuous woman and have children with her, for like an adulterous wife this land is guilty of unfaithfulness to the Lord." [Hosea 1: 2]*

Down through the ages, Noah, Abraham, Moses and David, we see God forgiving and offering another chance for mankind to return to Him. Finally, as God had Hosea do for Gomer, the Son departs His home in Heaven to travel to the far places we had gone to and found ourselves enslaved to sins of myriad types to purchase our redemption and freedom with His own blood.

The writer of Romans cited Hosea's example and God's counsel on why He had Hosea provide a human example of what God would be doing when the Messiah would come to walk with us.

> *"Even us, whom he also called, not only from the Jews but also from the Gentiles? As he says in Hosea: "I will call them 'my people' who are not my people; and I will call her 'my loved one' who is not my loved one," and, "In the very place where it was said to them, 'You are not my people,' there they will be called 'children of the living God." [Romans 9: 24-26 (NKJV)]*

So in the beyond customary forgiveness and loving Hosea was asked to demonstrate, we see the yearning love of our God that we should again reside in His house. It is a demonstration of the fulfillment of what is expected of a covenant keeper; that is to make all effort to bring the wandering party back into compliance.

In this prophetic book we see both sides of our relationship with God played out in human terms. We see the Covenant keeper and the Covenant breaker in what was meant to be an intimate and joyous union. Then we see our weaknesses followed by the extraordinary lengths the Covenant keeper is prepared to go in seeking the restoration. This example is provided for us in the first chapters of the Book of Hosea, and then in the last half of the book we see God's charges against Israel as covenant breakers. The last chapter in this book contains this offer to the wandering Covenant breakers.

> *"O Israel, come back! Return to your God! You're down but you're not out. Prepare your confession and come back to God. Pray to him, 'Take away our sin, accept our confession. Receive as restitution our repentant prayers. Assyria won't save us; horses won't get us where we want to go. We'll never again say 'our god' to something we've made or made up. You're our last hope. Is it not true that in you the orphan finds mercy?'" [Hosea 14: 1-3 MSG]*

Is this not what the Gospel would provide to humankind the world over? It calls us back, assures our acceptance and protection.

## Joel:

The entire book of Joel deals with the coming Day of the Lord. It speaks of both Advents of the Lord, from Joel's perspective it was hard if not impossible to distinguish between the first and second comings. The book begins with this wake-up call;

> *"Hear this, you elders; listen, all who live in the land. Has anything like this ever happened in your days or in the days of your ancestors?" [Joel 1: 1].*

It then continues with events from the first coming and the second coming intertwined throughout. We are only able to separate them now because we are between the two advents of the Messiah.

Joel chapter two gives us again a blended picture of the first and second advents of the Messiah. In it [Joel 2] we find the prophecy the Apostle Peter cited on the Day of Pentacost.

> *"And afterward, I will pour out my Spirit on all people. Your sons and daughters will prophesy, your old men will dream dreams, your young men will see visions." [Joel 2: 28]*

This is a picture of what would occur when the Holy Spirit was poured out. That event could only occur after the atoning sacrifice of Jesus had been completed with the resurrection. If the people remembered another verse from Joel 2 perhaps they quite possibly would have already been asking the followers of Christ for more information.

*"Before them the earth shakes, the heavens tremble, the sun and moon are darkened, and the stars no longer shine." [Joel 2: 10]*

For this is what is recorded in the Book of Matthew concerning the events on the day of the crucifixion of Jesus Christ.

*"From noon until three in the afternoon darkness came over all the land." [Matthew 27: 45]*

And

*"At that moment the curtain of the temple was torn in two from top to bottom. The earth shook, the rocks split and the tombs broke open. The bodies of many holy people who had died were raised to life." [Matthew 27: 51, 52]*

Again we find an intermingling throughout this chapter of the Book of Joel of the fulfilled prophesy and those things yet to come in the Day of the Lord.

## Jonah:

Christ, himself, cited the Prophet Jonah's sojourn in the great fish for three days as a sign that God's plan for the payment in full of the propitiation, redemption and atonement debts of sin had been satisfied. Then it gave us the timing that would happen in the spreading of the Gospel. Jonah was a prophet to Israel and it would be reasonable to think that prior to his call to go to Nineveh that he spoke to the Israelites on God's desires exclusively. Then due to

Jonah's reluctance to carry God's word to the Gentiles, God had him for three days contained below the sea in the belly of a whale. It was only after that sojourn that Jonah went out to the gentile nation of Nineveh to preach the word of God. The human Jonah was very reluctant to take this saving message to the Ninevites because they had a very wicked and viciously evil reputation in the known world at that time. Giving us the depth and breadth of God's willingness to forgive.

> *"As the crowds increased, Jesus said, "This is a wicked generation. It asks for a sign, but none will be given it except the sign of Jonah. For as Jonah was a sign to the Ninevites, so also will the Son of Man be to this generation." [Luke 11: 28-30]*

This citation of the Prophet Jonah should have called to mind the sequence that led to the spreading of God's word to the Gentiles. First the Word came to a man of the chosen people. Then this man was interred for three day and then was set free from interment. After this time the Word of God went to the sinning gentiles of Nineveh. So in this way Jonah prefigured the time that Christ would be in the grave before the resurrection and the subsequent spreading of the Gospel to the rest of the world. In that it was, also, a reaffirmation that the promised reconciliation was not only for the nation of Israel but also for the gentile world at large.

In Jonah's story again we see God's concern for all mankind not just the chosen people. In it is the reiteration of the promise given to Abraham, which said that out of Israel would come the blessing of shelter or salvation for the rest of the peoples of the world.

## Isaiah:

The Prophet Isaiah, perhaps, gives us the most complete picture of the Messiah. He gives us a description of how the Messiah would arrive and how He would be seen by many. Then an account of what He would endure to obtain our healing. Finally Isaiah gives us a glorious listing of His names and honors.

Isaiah tells us of his virgin birth, his wisdom and how he would appear to not conform to the norms as defined by the religious community.

> *"Then Isaiah said, "Hear now, you house of David! Is it not enough to try the patience of humans? Will you try the patience of my God also? Therefore the Lord himself will give you a sign: The virgin will conceive and give birth to a son, and will call him Immanuel. He will be eating curds and honey when he knows enough to reject the wrong and choose the right, for before the boy knows enough to reject the wrong and choose the right," [Isaiah 7: 13-15]*

In this passage we see that the Messiah would indeed come from the house of David, of a young girl. Then that His wisdom would be beyond His apparent years. It, also, indicates that at times what was held to be the normative would not hold while he was present with us. For example, when confronted by the priests about His disciple's lack of fasting and praying Jesus responded;

> *"Jesus answered, "Can you make the friends of the bridegroom fast while he is with them?" [Luke 5: 34, 35]*

Next is that oft recited passage from Isaiah, found in Isaiah chapter 53. Verse 5 says;

> *"But he was pierced for our transgressions, he was crushed for our iniquities; the punishment that brought us peace was on him, and by his wounds we are healed."*

If one looks at the entire chapter it paints the bleak picture of what it would cost Our Lord to pay for our redemption. It lists our rejection, our misperception that His affliction was of His own making, His fortitude and forbearance in not being accusatory of the ones who were the cause of His pain, it also lists several times the purpose for His coming, to seek out the lost and to provide a full price redemption.

As to the names and honors that are His, who does not know the list of his names and honors found in Isaiah 9? The list is found in verses 6 through 9 of that chapter.

> *"For to us a child is born, to us a son is given, and the government will be on his shoulders. And he will be called Wonderful Counselor, Mighty God, Everlasting Father, Prince of Peace. Of the greatness of his government and peace there will be no end. He will reign on David's throne and over his kingdom, establishing and upholding it with justice and righteousness from that time on and forever. The zeal of the Lord Almighty will accomplish this."*

This not only is a wonderfully reassuring list but it also indicates the unity of the triune God. For the Mighty God is, our Everlasting Father, the Prince of Peace bringing an offering by which we can obtain peace with God and the Wonderful Counselor who is with and within us today.

In Isaiah, there are several other references to the Messiah which makes this book one of the most complete pictures of the purpose, manner and costs placed on mankind's redemption and the reconciliation that God has been desirous of since the beginning. We, also, have his prophesy of the indwelling of the Holy Spirit that could only come after the fulfillment of the purpose of the first Advent of the Messiah. It is found in the fifty-ninth chapter verses 20 and 21.

> *"The Redeemer will come to Zion, to those in Jacob who repent of their sins," declares the Lord. "As for me, this is my covenant with them," says the Lord. "My Spirit, who is on you, will not depart from you, and my words that I have put in your mouth will always be on your lips, on the lips of your children and on the lips of their descendants – from this time on and forever," says the Lord."*

This is the Father telling us that our Redeemer will come and that then those who would repent could confidently expect the Holy Spirit would come to us and would not depart from them.

Then in the last chapter of Isaiah we see God's desire that not only would Israel welcome the Redeemer but that the message of redemption and inclusion be disseminated throughout the world. In the last verses of this book we see the gathering of all the people again under one God. First we see the continuity of God's desire and purpose in this chapter for in listing the languages groups of the gathered gentiles we hear echoes of those language groups created by God at the time of the scattering of the people as a consequence of Babel and whispers of those that would be evidence at Pentecost.

> For I know their works and their thoughts: it shall come, that I will gather all nations and tongues; and they shall come, and see my glory. [Isaiah 66: 18 KJV]

Later verses speak of the equality of the people who have chosen to respond, repent and return in their service before the altar of God in His holy city. So while Isaiah speaks mainly to the first advent of Christ, within it we find foreshadowing of the coming church age and the Second Advent.

## Jeremiah:

In Jeremiah we encounter again the problem that is all too easy to fall into, that being the foreshortening of events from our perspective. From Jeremiah's point in time several hundred years before Christ, he was given visions pertaining to the Messiah that are a mixture of what would happen when Christ would come to offer us the Grace of the Gospel, and what is yet to come when the End Time Kingdom will be established. Thus in Jeremiah we have the New Covenant which Christ set in force with Communion intermingled with prophesies of the Temple rebuilt and the establishment of the eternal Jerusalem. We now with the benefit of hindsight understand these prophecies to be a blending of two separate events.

When trying to discern what was the ordering of the events given in these prophesies there was great difficulty until the Messiah had come and had presented the gospel for the reconciliation. It was only then that we could see that there were two intertwined events that were part of the complete plan. Some belonging to the first advent that set in place the New Covenant that was necessary for the reestablishment of true temple worship in the New Jerusalem. This is very evident in chapter 31 of the Book of Jeremiah, where we see everything from Herod's slaughter of the innocents through the bringing of the New Covenant to the reestablishment of Temple worship ending in the New Jerusalem. So if one considered this prophesy to be all one event at one place in time, there might be confusion and doubts raised.

A most succinct statement of the coming Messiah in the first Advent is found in Jeremiah 33: 14-16 yet it also contains a foreshadowing of the final resumption of the Kingdom communion with God.

> *"The days are coming,' declares the Lord, 'when I will fulfill the good promise I made to the people of Israel and Judah. "In those days and at that time I will make a righteous Branch sprout from David's line; he will do what is just and right in the land. In those days Judah will be saved and Jerusalem will live in safety. This is the name by which it will be called: The Lord Our Righteous Savior."*

The first portion has come to pass and we are looking forward to the reunion when Judah and Jerusalem will live in safety under the rule of our Savior.

## Micah:

The prophesy from the prophet Micah, that is most well-known is the one quoted to King Herod by the chief priests and teachers of the law to answer the Magi's question about where the King of the Jews was to be born. In answer to the Gentiles seeking the Messiah, they cited the prophesy found in Micah 5: 2;

> *"But you, Bethlehem Ephrathah, though you are small among the clans of Judah, out of you will come for me one who will be ruler over Israel, whose origins are from of old, from ancient times."*

While there are few further details given about the coming of the Messiah in the book of Micah. In chapter 3, there is a rather stark prophesy as to what would befall Jerusalem when they rejected the Messiah. Micah 3 starts out in verse 1 with addressing the leadership and their ignoring God's justice;

> *"Listen, you leaders of Jacob, you rulers of Israel. Should you not embrace justice."*

Micah goes on in verse 4 to read out God's verdict for their failure to see and accept;

> *"Then they will cry out to the Lord, but he will not answer them. At that time he will hide his face from them because of the evil they have done."*

Then it ends in verse 12 with a prophesy on what would be the punishment;

> *"Therefore because of you, Zion will be plowed like a field, Jerusalem will become a heap of rubble, the temple hill a mound overgrown with thickets."*

In Jewish tradition there is a fast that is done annually in memory of the time when the Roman destruction of Jerusalem occurred, then it's being plowed to make way for the new Roman city to be constructed after the destruction of the Temple. [12] Not only was the Temple destroyed in 70 AD but then sixty-six years later to the day the area around the Temple was plowed under by the Roman General Turnus Rufus and Jews were banned from the new city. [13]

## Haggai:[14]

This is one of the shortest books in the Old Testament yet in it we find out which branch of David's descendants would bring us the Messiah. In the final verse of the book we are told;

> *"On that day, declares the Lord Almighty, 'I will take you, my servant Zerubbabel son of Shealtiel,' declares the Lord, 'and I will make you like my signet ring, for I have chosen you,' declares the Lord Almighty." [Haggai 2: 23]*

This is then repeated within the Gospel of Luke's genealogy of Jesus Christ.

---

[12] Dolphin, Lambert. 2013. *The Destruction of the Second Temple.* June 27. Accessed May 2015. http://www.templemount.org/destruct2.html

[13] Times, Messianic. 2014. *Tisha B'Av Israel and the Horrible, No Good, Very Bad Day.* 8 1. Accessed 5 23, 2015. http://www.mjaa.org/site/News2?id=9086&security=1.

[14] 2000 - 2014. *Abarim Publications: sources.* http://www.abarim-publications.com/Meaning/Haggai.html#.VUQu4PlViko.

> *"the son of Joanan, the son of Rhesa, the son of*
> *Zerubbabel, the son of Shealtiel," [Luke 3: 27]*

The other interesting thing about this prophet is his concern about the tardiness of God's people in reconstructing their temple. He spoke most of the priority that establishing God's place should have in the life of Israel over the mundane day to day concerns. When added to the meaning ascribed to the prophet's name. That meaning is 'one who is born on the Feast of Tabernacles'. It creates a picture of how we should order our priorities in our journeying with God and His proper place in our daily planning.

## Zechariah:

The prophet Zechariah spoke more about the coming Messiah than most of the other prophets. The only prophet to speak of the Messiah more than Zechariah was the prophet Isaiah. While Isaiah spoke mostly of the first coming of the Messiah, this prophet (Zechariah) has found the most echo and references in the last book of the Bible, Revelation. So between them is a fairly comprehensive picture of the New Covenant time period. Zechariah's concern with the Day of the Lord is most evident with these prophecies;

> *"Shout and be glad, Daughter of Zion. For I am coming, and I will live among you," declares the Lord. "Many nations will be joined with the Lord in that day and will become my people. I will live among you and you will know that the Lord Almighty has sent me to you." [Zechariah 2: 10, 11]*

This tells of time when the many nations of the world will choose the Lord and that He will be among us and known to us. It also alludes to it confirming Jesus's mission of the first advent had at the behest of the Lord Almighty. And then there is this prophesy of the destruction of those who come against His city and the sorrow of those who see the reality of the one they initially rejected.

> *"On that day I will set out to destroy all the nations that attack Jerusalem and I will pour out on the house of David and the inhabitants of Jerusalem a spirit of grace and supplication. They will look on me, the one they have pierced, and they will mourn for him as one mourns for an only child, and grieve bitterly for him as one grieves for a firstborn son" [Zechariah 12: 9, 10].*

In other recorded prophecies Zechariah describes the New Jerusalem (chapter 2) and a repentant Israel (chapter 3). This has led many to the opinion that he [Zechariah] was led to speak to the end of times [Day of the Lord] more than the first advent of the Messiah.

## Conclusion

Via the prophets, God gave us an almost complete picture of His plan of restoration. In some He told us how the Advents would occur. In others He elaborated on the Messiah's purpose in coming to us and what the Messiah would do while with us. He gave us the lineage that would produce the Messiah and his birthplace. Most of all an account was given of what would be offered, what it would cost and the manner by which this restitution would be accomplished. Then we are given glimpses of the interim between the offer and the final restoration of creation. Perhaps the most challenging part was the problem of perspective in seeing the separation of time that would be required between the Messiah's first advent to His second coming and our ultimate return.

## III. Commandments, Law & Custom

The Commandments and Laws are God's complete set instructions on what it means to be holy and acceptable to God. These are the standards needed for the perfection of presence, person, probity and proximity to enter God's sanctuary. It is a written listing of the standards and practices God expects of those who would desire to come into His presence. Recognizing our weaknesses; it also contains restitution payment instructions for making the appropriate repentance and atonement offerings that would be required when we failed to perfectly conform to the instructions of holiness. Just as in Eden God knew that in and of our own efforts we would be woefully incapable of the perfection needed, yet we would like the opportunity to try. Because He knew us so well, He provided us with the means and methods for atoning for these short comings. All this was to create in us a true appreciation of the immensity of His gift of substitutionary propitiation that our Redeemer would offer. This gift of Grace fulfilled all of mankind's debts, when the Messiah assumed responsibility for restitution in its entirety. The following selections from the Law are merely a few examples and not a complete exposition of each law and how it was to set Israel apart as the model for God's more excellent way.

Then there are the customs. These are the means this guidance and instruction were put into practice in daily life and the methods used for instructing others. These along with the entirety of God's commandments and laws, must needs be perfectly adhered to constantly and in every way if one was to enter into God's presence on their own merits. For in the Book of James we are cautioned that the number of infractions is not the important thing but the fact that we failed to maintain a perfection is what disqualifies us.

*"For whoever keeps the whole law and yet stumbles at just one point is guilty of breaking all of it." [James 2: 10]*

Just one failure breaks the required perfection thus it disqualifies one from obtaining access to God's presence.

There is emphasis on the equal application of the law on all. God's law states that within the territory of Israel, there was to be no difference of the application of the Law between Israelites and foreigners who wished to enjoy the benefits available.

*"A foreigner residing among you who wants to celebrate the Lord's Passover must have all the males in his household circumcised; then he may take part like one born in the land. No uncircumcised male may eat it. The same law applies both to the native-born and to the foreigner residing among you." [Exodus 12: 48, 49]*

This is reinforced under the New Covenant where all who would come to God were the same.

49

*"There is no difference between Jew and Gentile, for all have sinned and fall short of the glory of God, and all are justified freely by his grace through the redemption that came by Christ Jesus." [Romans 3: 22-24]*

So it is evident that all of us are equal before God's Law and in the words of the Psalmist;

*"For I know my transgressions, and my sin is always before me. Against you, you only, have I sinned and done what is evil in your sight; so you are right in your verdict and justified when you judge." [Psalm 51: 3, 4]*

For who among us has been perfect in obedience? For it has been said; to have "bent" one is the same as breaking all of them.

## Commandments:

The essential requirements and standards established by God for anyone who would desire to walk before Him. These are the basic Ten Commandments with which we are very familiar. These commandments are as eternal and immutable as is God's holiness. These are first found in the 20th chapter of the Book of Exodus and state:

*"And God spoke all these words:*

*1. "I am the Lord your God, who brought you out of Egypt, out of the land of slavery. You shall have no other gods before me.*

*2. "You shall not make for yourself an image in the form of anything in heaven above or on the earth beneath or in the waters below. You shall not bow down to them or worship them; for I, the Lord your God, am a jealous God, punishing the children for the sin of the parents to the third and fourth generation of those who hate me, but showing love to a thousand generations of those who love me and keep my commandments.*

*3. "You shall not misuse the name of the Lord your God, for the Lord will not hold anyone guiltless who misuses his name.*

*4. "Remember the Sabbath day by keeping it holy. Six days you shall labor and do all your work, but the seventh day is a Sabbath to the Lord your God. On it you shall not do any work, neither you, nor your son or daughter, nor your male or female servant, nor your animals, nor any foreigner residing in your towns. For in six days the Lord made the heavens and the earth, the sea, and all that is in them, but he rested on the seventh day. Therefore the Lord blessed the Sabbath day and made it holy.*

*5. "Honor your father and your mother, so that you may live long in the land the Lord your God is giving you.*

*6. "You shall not murder.*

*7. "You shall not commit adultery.*

51

*Susan E. Craig*

8. *"You shall not steal.*

9. *"You shall not give false testimony against your neighbor.*

10. *"You shall not covet your neighbor's house. You shall not covet your neighbor's wife, or his male or female servant, his ox or donkey, or anything that belongs to your neighbor." [Verses 1-17]*

When trying to maintain God's standards many of us would say that we have not violated most of these, yet struggle with things like the "white lie". I contend though that the one that gives the most grief is allowing idols to creep into our lives. For it is very easy to become absorbed to distraction in the things, relationships, pleasures and worldly accolades so that they take precedence to considering the wonders of our Lord God.

## Laws:

Laws were given for the day to day living of walking with God in community with others. While the death penalty, that was part of the Law as the just consequence of violating the standards for righteousness and holiness, has now been waived under the offered pardon of Grace, God's standards and requirements have not been waived. So while some of these standards and requirements might run counter to our changing desires and inclinations; God has not, will not and can not change. Jesus affirmed this when He said;

*"Do not think that I have come to abolish the Law or the Prophets; I have not come to abolish them but to fulfill them. For truly I tell you, until heaven and earth disappear, not the smallest letter, not the least stroke of a pen, will by any means disappear from the Law until everything is accomplished. [Matthew 5: 17-18]*

However, He has placed before us the gift of complete pardon that allows us to escape the just consequences of our bad choices. He still desires us to strive to live the life that is best suited for His creation.

These are God's given instructions for day-to-day standard of conduct and dealings. These are so we are given ways of demonstrate in our daily walk His character, desires and requirements. They are designed to demonstrate what perfection was and should be again. It was to a practical example before the world. This example of God and the blessings of His ways were to be an attractive picture before the world in order that those who did not know Him would desire to find out.

It is the pattern we still strive to attain as we walk before Him. It contains teachings on personal health and nutrition, some of these have changed as we have increased our knowledge of food preservation and preparation. Yet even today modern medicine still discovers that much of the instructions given at the first, still have validity. One of those counsels that currently applies is the advisability for moderation in all things. Throughout the Bible, this is one admonishment God constantly reiterates.

*"Listen, my son, and be wise, and set your heart on the right path: do not join those who drink too much wine or gorge themselves on meat, for drunkards*

*and gluttons become poor, and drowsiness clothes
them in rags." [Proverbs 23: 19-21]*

Another thing that the Bible is insistent on is the act of forgiveness. It has been "discovered" that those who truly forgive have a greater sense of peace within themselves and possibly longer lives, plus reductions in blood pressure and overall stress levels[15]. The Law covers the means and methods for obtaining and giving forgiveness. Restitution is central to obtaining forgiveness for one's own errors or sins. God made instruction for what He'd consider adequate restitutions. This is done through the various Sin and Trespass offerings and sacrifices that God instituted for differing errors either intentional or by ignorance. It should be pointed out that restitution is to be worked out horizontally between our fellows and then vertically with God.

> *"Therefore, if you are offering your gift at the altar
> and there remember that your brother or sister has
> something against you, leave your gift there in
> front of the altar. First go and be reconciled to them;
> then come and offer your gift. [Matthew 5: 23, 24]*

This instruction emphasizes our need to deal rightly with our neighbors in our efforts to walk uprightly before God.

It is in these Laws that we, if we look, can see the functions and costs involved with the coming Savior. It, also, tells us of the debt consequences that we each, individually, would be required to pay to our Creator without the Grace that would be provided by the Messiah. It could be that

---

[15] Chan, Amanda L. 2014. *8 Ways Forgiveness Is Good For Your Health.* 10 26. Accessed 5 20, 2015 http.//huffingtonpost.com/ 2014/10/25 / forgiveness-health-benefits_n_6029736.html. .

since the Savior has come and made an all sufficient restitution for our debts and sins that some of the more unsettling requirements of the Law are no longer needed. However forgiveness remains an important principle. For it (forgiveness) features prominently in the prayer that Christ has taught us to pray. Under the Old Covenant forgiveness, from God, was obtained through sacrifices for restitution and atonement. Another convention that thankfully we no longer have to administer is the proscribed death penalties for violating the Law in order to attempt to maintain the standards required for righteousness and holiness before God. Others are strict exemplars of the hard things required to be totally blameless before God; of these laws it is grace that God does not expect our perfect obedience. But He does expect the recognition on our part that such an infraction has occurred. This is to be followed by confession and repentance from those things which would cause us to be separated were it not for the Grace offered through Christ.

## Social dealings:

As God is desirous of a community with man, he has given us the parameters of what such a community should look like. These are found in the laws pertaining to relational dealings of day to day living. Building out from the family to eventually encompass how we are to deal with those who either do not know or have rejected God. This is not to say that at any time has man been able to conform entirely to any of these guidelines. We come up short time and again for it is very easy to think first of one's self before considering others no matter how closely related to us they may or may not be.

## Family:

Starting with the 5th Commandment for honoring our father and mother. It says nothing about the father or mother being worthy of that honor but that the station that they are in is worthy of being honored as an honorable office to hold. But it does say that in the honoring them it may go well in our lives. For as the Apostle Paul reminds us:

> "Children, obey your parents in the Lord, for this is right. Honor your father and mother — which is the first commandment with a promise — so that it may go well with you and that you may enjoy long life on the earth." [Ephesians 6: 1-3]

Conversely parents were to consider ways to teach their children so that struggles of life could effectively be met. This does not mean to protect them from the consequences entirely but to point them in the directions that are good and proper. It requires that they be taught to discern between what is good and what only appears good. Parents are to encourage their children to desire God's smiles over the accolades of the world around them.

> "Discipline your children, for in that there is hope; do not be a willing party to their death. A hot-tempered person must pay the penalty; rescue them, and you will have to do it again." [Proverbs 19: 18, 19].

Caution is then given to warn against creating antagonism in children to the instructions of God and their parents. For this antagonism tends to spill over into many other areas of parental beliefs. This links to the cautions given to those who teach to not lead astray their students by false teachings.

> *"Parents do not exasperate your children; instead, bring them up in the training and instruction of the Lord." [Ephesians 6: 4]*

As we are all God's children these also give us a good idea of how God will deal with us in our upbringing and discipline.

## Community:

Here are just two of the many instructions on how we are to deal with those around us. The first is how we are to deal fairly and honestly with our neighbors. The second is how we are to share our abundance with those who are struggling.

> *"Do not defraud or rob your neighbor. Do not hold back the wages of a hired worker overnight. Do not curse the deaf or put a stumbling block in front of the blind, but fear your God. I am the Lord." [Leviticus 19: 13, 14]*

And we are, also, instructed to share the bounty of God's provision with those less fortunate.

> *"When you reap the harvest of your land, do not reap to the very edges of your field or gather the gleanings of your harvest. Do not go over your vineyard a second time or pick up the grapes that have fallen.*

> Leave them for the poor and the foreigner. I am the
> Lord your God." [Leviticus 19: 9, 10]

As in main part we are no longer an agrarian society, perhaps we should look at our fields of labor in this light, not using solely for ourselves the fruits we obtain.

## World:

Many of the Laws that were given, also carried the instruction to treat others as they would have wished to have been treated when they were under Egyptian rule. This caution is found not only within the Books known as the Law. But it is found in other Books of the Bible notably Psalms, Ecclesiastes, Mark, and Luke.

> "Do not mistreat or oppress a foreigner, for you
> were foreigners in Egypt." [Exodus 22: 21]

In Luke, this is condensed for how we should treat people across the entire spectrum of humanity.

> "Do to others as you would have them do to you."
> [Luke 6: 31]

It is so close to God's heart that this reminder is repeated many places throughout the Law, the Hebrew people were instructed to treat strangers compassionately and justly. This is reiterated in Jesus' statement of the Law and Commandments and illustrated by the parable of the Good Samaritan.

> "Teacher, which is the greatest commandment in
> the Law?" Jesus replied: "'Love the Lord your God

*with all your heart and with all your soul and
with all your mind.' This is the first and greatest
commandment. And the second is like it: 'Love
your neighbor as yourself.' All the Law and the
Prophets hang on these two commandments."*
*[Matthew 22: 36-40]*

This is to be done with the same compassion and justice
they would treat the less fortunate of their own. An example
of this is found in Deuteronomy 24 verses 17 and 18;

*"Do not deprive the foreigner or the fatherless of
justice, or take the cloak of the widow as a pledge.
Remember that you were slaves in Egypt and the
Lord your God redeemed you from there. That is
why I command you to do this."*

For international relations there is this caution that is
found in Deuteronomy:

*"Give the people these orders: 'You are about to
pass through the territory of your relatives the
descendants of Esau, who live in Seir. They will be
afraid of you, but be very careful. Do not provoke
them to war, for I will not give you any of their
land, not even enough to put your foot on. I have
given Esau the hill country of Seir as his own.
You are to pay them in silver for the food you eat
and the water you drink.'" [Deuteronomy 2: 4-6]*

As we are all of God's creation, we can all said to be
relatives. Then, too, when we enter into business with
another we can be said to be passing through "their country".
So the instructions given can be and should be extrapolated

into daily life. In many ways as we come into contact with others in daily commerce, we are met with suspicion if not outright fear.

## Financial dealing:

As God knew that one of the tools of daily life would be the cause of much sorrow, He set forth the means and rules that would help us keep it under control. He has given us two well-known cautions. The first in Proverbs 22: 7;

> *"The rich rule over the poor, and the borrower is slave to the lender".*

This insight shows that the ones who look to others for provision are compelled to abide in what the provider stipulates. The second warns that this tool could come to supplant God in the hearts and minds of man becoming an idol that many would worship. This warning is found in 1 Timothy 6: 9, 10 and is misquoted often leaving out the key words in the passage (love of). It reads;

> *"Those who want to get rich fall into temptation and a trap and into many foolish and harmful desires that plunge people into ruin and destruction. For the love of money is a root of all kinds of evil. Some people, eager for money, have wandered from the faith and pierced themselves with many griefs."*

Many try to shift the blame onto the tool away from their own hearts love of money and the things they think it will bring. This sets the tool [money] up as an idol to be bowed down to in their lives.

**Community:**

Many provisions were made for the protection and assistance of those in the community who were in need. The best known of these is the provisions for the needy called gleaning. This left a portion of the harvest yield for those people to go and gather food for themselves and their families with no shame or obligation to the land owner. Note this also gave dignity of effort to the one in need. Then there is instruction for dealing with a fellow believer who falls on hard times.

> *"If any of your fellow Israelites become poor and are unable to support themselves among you, help them as you would a foreigner and stranger, so they can continue to live among you. Do not take interest or any profit from them, but fear your God, so that they may continue to live among you." [Leviticus 25: 35, 36]*

Another instance can be found in the instructions for charity along with the encouragement to provide this assistance with the least amount of fanfare as possible.

> *"If anyone is poor among your fellow Israelites in any of the towns of the land the Lord your God is giving you, do not be hardhearted or tightfisted toward them. Rather, be openhanded and freely lend them whatever they need. Be careful not to harbor this wicked thought: "The seventh year, the year for canceling debts, is near," so that you do not show ill will toward the needy among your fellow Israelites and give them nothing. They may then appeal to the Lord against you, and you*

*will be found guilty of sin. Give generously to them and do so without a grudging heart; then because of this the Lord your God will bless you in all your work and in everything you put your hand to. There will always be poor people in the land. Therefore I command you to be openhanded toward your fellow Israelites who are poor and needy in your land." [Deuteronomy 15: 7-11]*

This is reinforced in the New Testament instruction:

*"So when you give to the needy, do not announce it with trumpets, as the hypocrites do in the synagogues and on the streets, to be honored by others. Truly I tell you, they have received their reward in full. But when you give to the needy, do not let your left hand know what your right hand is doing, so that your giving may be in secret. Then your Father, who sees what is done in secret, will reward you." [Matthew 6: 2-4]*

So while we are encouraged to consider the needs of others we are to do this discreetly and with consideration of the feelings of the ones being helped. We do not need the accolades of those around us for the God who loves us knows without the advertisement.

## World:

God wants His people to picture his honor, integrity and truth. So as we deal with the world we are not to change His standards.

*"'Do not use dishonest standards when measuring length, weight or quantity. Use honest scales and honest weights, an honest ephah and an honest hin I am the Lord your God, who brought you out of Egypt. [Leviticus 19: 35, 36]*

In the New Testament this is extended in two of Jesus's teachings.

*"All you need to say is simply 'Yes' or 'No'; anything beyond this comes from the evil one.." [Matthew 5: 37]*

*"Do not judge, or you too will be judged. For in the same way you judge others, you will be judged, and with the measure you use, it will be measured to you." [Matthew 7: 1, 2].*

These are indications that God expects and wants honesty and consistency from us in all of our dealings. It shows us as well that the criteria we use to discern and make assessments will be used by those watching us to measure our faithfulness and integrity.

There are also instructions to those who will be in positions of power or rule over others. These are instructed to, not only, to not consider themselves better than those they rule over but also reminds the ruler that he is not above the law;

*"It [the Law] is to be with him, and he is to read it all the days of his life so that he may learn to revere the Lord his God and follow carefully all the words of this law and these decrees and not consider himself better than his fellow Israelites*

*and turn from the law to the right or to the left."*
*[Deuteronomy 17: 19, 20]*

This points to the servant nature of leadership that Christ modeled for us through His life, death and resurrection. It is how we to this day should look at positions of power.

These are just a few examples from the Books of the Law of the standards God desires His people to strive to uphold.

## Sabbath, Sabbatical & Jubilee years:

Then there are the instructions for rest, restoration and redemption to be done at set intervals. These were just some of the many instructions contained in the law that were to set the Israelites apart from those around them. These practices were as foreshadowing pictures of the rest, forgiveness and restoration that are found in God's ways. The Sabbath a day of rest for all men regardless of station in life or standing in the community. The Sabbatical year given for the rejuvenation of all in the land and included the land which was to lie fallow during that year. During the Sabbatical year, those who had entered into slavery for reasons of indebtedness were to be offered their freedom. The culmination of this series of three provisions for the well-being of man, beast and land was to be the year of Jubilee which was the year of restoration to original standing and holdings, forgiveness of debts that had caused forfeiture of holding or freedoms and it included rest for the land as it was celebrated as the seventh Sabbatical year. One of the main features of the Year of Jubilee was the manumission of all slaves. During the Year of Jubilee God promised that his provision for all would be sufficient throughout the entire year. Unfortunately the last of these established events was largely ignored throughout history for all too human of reasonings.

The instructions for these events and celebrations can be found in the books of Exodus, Leviticus, Numbers and Deuteronomy.

- Sabbath – Exodus 16 through 20, Leviticus 16 through 35, Numbers 15 to 28, and Deuteronomy 5.
- Sabbatical – Exodus 23, Leviticus 25 to 26, and Numbers 26 to 28.
- Year of Jubilee – Leviticus 25 to 27, and Numbers 36.

## Custom:

Custom is the daily usage and understanding of what is right and proper. Not only was the society established under God's directions to be a unique demonstration of His love and grace. But there was another way it was very different from other peoples. This is because the language symbols in which its structure was communicated from God is one in which there is a completeness and a total unity. For not only is it designed to communicate verbally but it also functions numerically and musically[16]. So not only can we learn how we are to behave in our daily walk, we can sing it in our hearts and to the world and, also, we are given a way to measure it. Custom is how we put the instructions of the Commandments and Law into daily practice. It is one good method of transmittal; but it also can cause conflict with following generations. This occurs when there is a rigidity to it without explanations of the how and why things came to be done the way they are, so understanding is essential.

---

[16] Wheeler, John. 2015. *Music of the Bible Revealed.* June 25. Accessed July 9, 2015. http://www.rakkav.com/biblemusic/pages/suzanne.htm.

As language and numbers are things that are ubiquitous in daily life. In Hebrew the characters for language and numbering are one and the same, it gives a unity not found elsewhere when the language symbols and number symbols in use are distinctly different. Now that we've recently have rediscovered that these very same symbols given to transmit God's instruction and counsel also are musical notations. Think of it, not only can we exchange ideas and understanding, but also have a measure against which to assess things and bring them to harmony in one complete symbol. All while being reminded of God's presence.

In the language God used to communicate with man it has developed that certain numbers carry symbolic meaning to the community. The some of these numbers are three, four, seven, twelve and forty have a significance within God's order. Of the numbers that have significant implications here are four of them and some of the meanings that have been ascribed to them. The first that comes to mind is the number seven (7); which carries connotations of spiritual perfection or submission in addition to a meanings of divine fullness, completeness and totality. The second is three (3) which significantly has connotations of truth and mediated reconciliation. Then there is the number four (4) for which there are aspects of solidity, universality and creation. We carry the connotation of solid permanence in the saying "four square". Then taking 4 times 10, we get 40 which reoccurs frequently through the Bible in conjunction with times of testing, purification, and for establishing a habit. All this to say that custom can and does carry a depth of meaning that adds to the language.

Custom can be found in the monuments we erect and celebrations we hold, too. For originally these were created to commemorate something significant in the lives of the nation or community. Biblically commemorated celebrations were established to teach something significant in the journey of return. There were six celebrations, feasts or festivals that God gave in the cycle of a year. They are in order; Passover [forgiveness], Unleavened Bread [cleansing from sin], Weeks [giving of the Law/indwelling of the Holy Spirit], Trumpets [redemption and restoration], Atonement [reconciliation] and Tabernacles [ingathering]. If one gets caught up in the trappings and other surface expressions; the purpose of these customs [that is to transmit a significant event or principle] can be lost over time. In modern times we see this loss most in our three most celebrated holidays; Thanksgiving, Christmas and Easter.

## III. Conclusion:

God used the Commandments and Law in two ways. The first being to give us a picture and understanding of what it means to be completely righteous and holy and thus fit to be his companions. Then secondly, though it is the primary reason, the Law was to be the means for man to come to know how utterly incapable he could be of maintaining the perfection required to safely and confidently to enter into God's presence. Once we could understand that in our own strength we cannot maintain perfection of presence, person, probity and proximity we could comprehend the graciousness of the gift of God's Grace. Leading to a recognition of our need for the magnificent gift that Grace is and to be ready and willing to accept the proffered freedom. The Apostle Paul says this in his exposition of faith to the Romans;

*"Therefore no one will be declared righteous in God's sight by the works of the law; rather, through the law we become conscious of our sin."*
*[Romans 3: 20]*

He instructed us to erect monuments and hold festivals as a customary way for us to transmit through the generations the memory of His provision, guidance and love. They were above all to be teaching tools for us to use. As God instructed Joshua at the time when the children of Israel crossed the Jordan River and subsequently as the Israelites proceeded into the Promised Land on several occasions to erect stones of remembrance.

*"So Joshua called together the twelve men he had appointed from the Israelites, one from each tribe, and said to them, "Go over before the ark of the Lord your God into the middle of the Jordan. Each of you is to take up a stone on his shoulder, according to the number of the tribes of the Israelites, to serve as a sign among you. In the future, when your children ask you, 'What do these stones mean?' tell them that the flow of the Jordan was cut off before the ark of the covenant of the Lord. When it crossed the Jordan, the waters of the Jordan were cut off. These stones are to be a memorial to the people of Israel forever." [Joshua 4: 4-7]*

So it might be helpful to erect our own milestones and monuments to commemorate God's loving kindnesses to us along our journey.

The Commandments and Laws therefore are descriptions of who and what God is. They are a listing of the requirements needed to sustain the perfect holiness surrounding God. For those who love God and study to please Him they are guides to what is most pleasing to Him for in no way would we wish to diminish the glory and honors of our beloved. It is a blessing that He has given us a covering for those times we fail in our understanding and performance.

In the festivals instituted by God for the yearly cycle of worship for the Hebrew people we find that the cycle patterned the process of reunion that has significance today. They are to be teaching tools for subsequent generations as we pass along the meaning and significance of these celebrations. The feast of Tabernacles commemorates the time when God traveled with them as he led them to the home He had appointed for them. The feast of Tabernacles, also, celebrates God's ingathering of His people to the home he had established for them. It serves as a reminder of His desire to be intimately involved with them, His dwelling and travelling with them and finally His provision for them along the way. As such it can be seen as what we can expect as we look forward to on our journey toward the final ingathering that will come with the New Heavens and earth.

# CHAPTER 5

———•———

## Summary of the Plan for Our Restoration

So just as no teacher would start five year old students starting to learn mathematics immediately with instructions in calculus computations, so God has stepped us first through a realization of what had been left behind. The next lesson, to be presented, was the lesson on what it meant to be holy and the requirements and standards needed to achieve this state of holy righteousness. At this time there was a reiteration of the promise that should we discover we needed help to become a holy righteous people help would be provided. Then He has lead us through the process by which we can make the return. Just as happened before the first Advent we have been given signposts that we should look for along the way.

Through the covenants increasing specificity the stepped process towards restoring the communion and intimacy of the relationship we had was set out and promised. Each perfectly setting up the next step towards our reconciliation with God. God's initial gift of free will remains and God will not violate His word nor rescind His giving. Because of this, we now confidently hope for the time when our Lord will tabernacle face to face with His people eternally. For now we have the opportunity choose tabernacling with the Holy Spirit. For God promised His Comforter to come reside within us comforting, counselling, and guiding us. We should therefore carefully attend to our Tabernacles.

In the prophets, we are given an almost complete picture of His plan of restoration. Some told of how the Advents would occur. While others elaborated on what would happen during the first Advent. The lineage that would produce the Messiah and his birthplace were pinpointed. An accounting was given of what would be offered and what it would cost. Mixed throughout were given glimpses of the interim between the initial offering and the events of the final restoration of creation.

As a vital part of our understanding of the requirements needed to come into His Holy presence; He gave us the Commandments and Law. These served two purposes. The Law is God's teaching to give us a way to understand what complete holiness and righteousness entails. Thus instructing in what it means to be fit companions able to stand in His presence. The primary reason, though, the Law was to be the means for man to see how utterly incapable he is of maintaining the perfection required to safely and confidently to enter into God's presence. Thus preparing us to accept the magnificent gift of His Grace. The Commandments and Laws therefore are descriptions of who and what God is.

He gave aids to our memory so that we could accurately transmit all that His provision, guidance and love had done for us. So it might be good to continue this custom of erecting milestones to commemorate God's loving kindnesses along our journey.

Lastly, in the festivals instituted by God for the yearly cycle of worship is found the pattern of the process of our reunion with God. It is in the last of these feasts, the feast of Tabernacles, which commemorates the time when God called His people out as His own and walked with them daily as He brought them to the home He had set aside for them that we see His desire for our continued walk with Him. The celebration of that first ingathering is a reassurance of what God has promised will come eventually. God had promised to Abraham and Jacob that they would be established in a land of their own. Thus it serves also as guarantor to His promise to dwell and walk with us as He prepares us and the home he has promised.

Perhaps some of this was part of the instruction Jesus gave to the mourning disciples on the road to Emmaus concerning himself and the plan of salvation. This event has long been a curiosity to me, as I would dearly love to have heard the instruction they received from Jesus, that day.

> *"He said to them, "How foolish you are, and how slow to believe all that the prophets have spoken! Did not the Messiah have to suffer these things and then enter his glory?" And beginning with Moses and all the Prophets, he explained to them what was said in all the Scriptures concerning himself." [Luke 24: 25 -27]*

Now in this day, we have been offered the help promised and the covering has been provided for where we have fallen so woefully short of the mark set by Gods standards for holiness. Now, it is for us to seek out and accept this proffered gift. This has been provided because God greatly desires that we may safely enter into His presence and to renew our union with Him. So as we continue on our journey home again to our loving Creator the roadmap is in our hands. Let us look at what was instructed once before, when God gathered His people to Himself into a specific place. Seeing what that time of ingathering can tell us about preparing, serving and worshipping in our own tabernacles. For this is the time of God's second ingathering.

At the time of this ingathering God still answers the question asked in Psalm 15, with an invitation to any and all who will come unto Him, humbly accepting the gift the Son.

*"Lord, who shall abide in thy tabernacle? Who shall dwell in thy holy hill? [Psalms 15: 1 KJV]*

# CHAPTER 6

———✦———

## Festival of Tabernacles[17]

The Festival of Tabernacles is the third of the fall festivals that run from the first day of the seventh month through the 22nd day. The first in order is the Festival of the Trumpets (redemption) celebrated on the first day of the month. This festival is a reminder of everything that is contained in the promises of the Sabbath, the Sabbatical year, and the Year of Jubilee. The second festival day is on the 10th of that month and is The Day of Atonement (reconciliation). The days between these two are traditionally called the "Days of Awe". This was a reminder of the debt owed to God and the cost of the restitution to be made. The final of the yearly festivals is the seven day Festival of Tabernacles (ingathering and thanksgiving) and commences on the 15th of the month and runs for 7 days. Commemorating the time God gathered his people from slavery, walked with them on the journey to the home He had established for them. So in the order of the end of the yearly commanded Festivals we

---

[17] Parsons, John J. 2003. *The Festival of Sukkot - the Feast of Tabernacles.* Accessed June 2, 2015. http://www.hebrew4christians.com/ Holidays/Fall_Holidays/Sukkot/sukkot.html.

see days celebrating forgiveness and redemption leading to the reconciliation, then culminating in a week-long celebration of thanksgiving and God's ingathering. The instructions for this commemorative festival are found in Leviticus 23: 33-43.

In modern Judaism the festival runs for 8 or 9 days, the difference in length depends on your location. If one is in Israel it is 8 days but if you are part of the diaspora, the celebration runs 9 days. There are two traditional blessings that are recited at the time of the festival. This is recited at the start of the festival - "Blessed are you, Lord our God, Master of the Universe, who has kept us alive and sustained us, and brought us to this special time."; and then this just before the meal each night - "Sanctify us who, King of the Universe our God, LORD, you blessed in the Tabernacle to dwell and commanded with the Law".

Another title for this time is the "Season of our Joy". It is interesting that in Bible instructions for the three commanded festivals [Passover, First Fruits, and Tabernacles] the word for joy increases in frequency within the feast instructions from first to last. For Passover the word is not mentioned, within the instructions for First Fruits there is one mention, but it is found several times throughout the directions for celebrating the Festival of Tabernacles.

So this festival reminds us that God in His wisdom and love has brought in and will again bring in a harvest and will cause us to dwell again in His tents. It is a celebration of our and God's joy at the anticipated restoration and reunion. Until that time he sends us the comfort of the Holy Spirit to travel with us in our tents to the home that is being prepared for us.

# CHAPTER 7

Old Testament Tabernacle/Temple

The concept of tabernacle is mainly used as a noun and defined in modern usage as a receptacle for the consecrated things, or a house of worship. In Bible times it was a temporary movable dwelling place. Is this not an apt description of the believer? We are to be consecrated vessels into which God pours his love and blessing. Also, we are told over and over that our sojourn in our earthly form is a temporary one. We are foreigners who travel here for a while (fulfilling His purposes) as we journey towards our Heavenly Father and true home. While on this journey God, as He has promised, will dwell with and within us.

This then leads to consideration of His instructions for the construction, furnishing, serving in and maintenance of the Tabernacle for Him when he was ingathering His people and bringing them home to Israel. In that it could be a pattern for our daily walk with God. For each of now carries in himself a tabernacle where God the Holy Spirit has come to reside with each believer as we travel to our heavenly home. As we desire God's guidance, counsel and comfort we should strive to maintain our Tabernacle in as good an order as we can. Guarding against the establishment of idols that would grieve the Holy Spirit.

The Tabernacle is the place where the believer would go to meet with God for fellowship, guidance, solace and love. During the Ingathering of the Israelites to their Promised Land, it consisted of a three part structure. The outer precinct which surrounded the Tent of Meeting was for community worship and contained the High Altar for burnt sacrifices. Then there was the Tent of Meeting which consisted of two chambers, the Inner Court and the Holy of Holies. It had specific structure, adornments in addition to restrictions as to who could enter the different portions. There, also, were very specific conditions and rituals needed to enter each portion. One of the conditions that went away with the institution of the New Covenant were the restricted times when access to God's the Tent of Meeting and the Holy of Holies. Now we can approach at any time we are so inclined or feel a need. Under the new covenant, each individual has the privilege to withdraw into private communing with God in their very own tent. As the Apostle Peter said in the book 2 Peter 1: 12 and 13,

> *"So I will always remind you of these things, even though you know them and are firmly established in the truth you now have. I think it is right to refresh your memory as long as I live in the tent of this body".*

In the Old Covenant – the temple or tabernacle had a specific geographic location where God's glory was present and where man came to interact and receive instruction in God's precepts for righteousness and right living. God instructed the Hebrews through Moses as to the precise specifications of its structure and adornment. Each of these things carried meaning and instruction. The structure had three portions and the accoutrements for each "room" within the Tabernacle were specific to the purpose and meaning of that room. When the Temple was constructed a Court of the Gentiles was added where those who did not fulfill the requirements to proceed further could come to learn about God.

## I. Holy of Holies within the Tent of Meeting

The Tent of Meeting had two chambers. The most holy portion was called the Holy of Holies and was the place or seat of God's presence. Access to the Holy of Holies and the Inner Court, until the provision of grace, was restricted to only those designated as intermediaries. To proceed from the Inner Court into the Holy of Holies was further restricted to the High Priest and only for the length of his tenure in that position. Special preparations by the designated intermediaries were needed before they could approach beyond the each veil. Even then if all preparatory steps were appropriately done or there was something the high-priest had hidden it could be fatal for the High Priest to continue inside the second veil. Temple records and custom has it that a cord was tied to the ankle and bells were on the robes so that if the bells fell silent those outside the veil could pull the high-priest's body from the Holy of Holies.

## Specifications:

The Tent of Meeting was to be taller than the surrounding structures so that all could see it and be reassured that God was there with them, for it was from the Holy of Holies that the Shekainah glory emanated. It was sectioned off into two rooms, one where the daily offerings of Shewbread, drink and incense were placed, it was constantly lit with oil lamps; and then there was the Holy of Holies, that portion which was reserved solely for God's presence. This room was where the Ark of the Covenant and the Mercy Seat were placed and the Cherubim stood watch. This second portion of the Tent of Meeting was entered only by the High Priest bringing the blood offerings and then only on specified occasions.

- Lofty rising above the surrounding community so as to be visible from afar. It was three times as long as it was wide.
- Colors – blue, for the heavens, purity and truth: purple, for royalty and riches; & scarlet, has connotations for blood, sin and divine retribution.
- Acacia wood – this wood has a symbolic meaning of overcoming death due to the wood's durability and hardness. It reminds us that in God we can overcome death through Christ's sacrifice and the offering of God's grace.
- Curtained off – while in many pagan religions the uninitiated were not likely permitted approach to the most "sacred" precinct of their temples, these were on display through openings and archways. God however was not on display to the general public. It created a separation between the defiled and the holy. This was a visible reminder of the unworthiness and debt man has in his desire to approach God. There were two curtains one at the entry to the Tent of Meeting and the second interior veil that separated the Inner Court from the Holy of Holies. The first blocked the way of the general

populace and the non-priestly Levites. Only those who were approved as intercessors could proceed beyond that curtain. The second stopped all but the ritually prepared High Priest who was substitution and intercessor for the entire tribe of Israel

- The entire Tent of meeting had four coverings. The first was fine linen representing righteousness. The second was made of goat hair symbolic of sin offering. The third was red dyed leather from rams hide. This was to signify substitution. And lastly there was a covering translated as badger skin symbolizing protection.[18]

## Furnishing of the Holy of Holies:

- Mercy Seat – this was a gold covering that was placed on the Ark of the Covenant where God would meet with the approved intermediary of the Israelites.
- Ark of the Covenant – the base on which the Mercy Seat was found. It contained the tablets of the Law that are God's standards; Aaron's rod that budded symbolic of the blossoming that comes with reconciliation with God; lastly, a container of Manna symbolic of God's provision and grace.
- Cherubim – were a portion of the gold covering of the Ark on either end. They were standing guard at the Mercy Seat combining the senses of justice and mercy all the while protecting the purity and holiness guarding the access route to reunion with God.

---

[18] n.d. *Covering of the Sanctuary.* Accessed April 2015. http://www.templebuildersministry.com/Index_Tabernacle_of_Moses_6.php.

## IV. Inner Court of the Tent of Meeting

These are the furnishings that are found outside the Holy of Holies but within the Inner Court of the Tent of Meeting. This area was accessible to the general priesthood. It was to be furnished with lamps and tables and adorned with gold, silver and gemstones. These were to be attended to continuously.

- Lampstand and Lamps – God's presence and word are the light of the world and are meant to shine continuously before all men. Seven golden lamps on a stand made of gold fashioned with flowers and buds. All implements for tending the lamps were to be made of gold as well.
- Table of acacia wood overlaid with gold on which were placed the 12 cakes of the bread of presence was to be kept supplied continually as well as bowls for poured out offerings. This was called the Table of presence and on it were placed the containers for the drink and bread to be shared before God.
- Altar of incense – called the golden altar as it was made of acacia wood overlaid with gold. It had four horns on the corners. It was placed before the curtain of separation on which only incense was to be burned continually and that only of a certain specification

This entire two chamber structure was called the tent of meeting. This was where God would meet with the designated and approved representative of His people. There was a curtain at the entrance to the tent and another curtain separating the Holy of Holies from the rest of the tent of meeting.

With the rending of the curtain that had separated the Holy of Holies from general access, all those who call upon Jesus as their savior and have received the covering He offered; these are granted access before the Mercy Seat. Whereas previously no one except the High Priest were permitted to enter. This access was permitted only once a year under very restricted conditions. The separating curtain was torn from top to bottom and occurred at the moment Christ fulfilled all righteous debts. This was to signify that this access was made possible solely by God and not by any effort on the part of mankind. Now all those in Christ can now confidently enter in without fear before the Mercy Seat and seek our Abba Father's counsel and reassurance. We are capable of serving before God as in Christ we are now a royal priesthood under the great high priest the Lord Jesus Christ.

*"But you are a chosen people, a royal priesthood,*
*a holy nation, God's special possession, that you*
*may declare the praises of him who called you out*
*of darkness into his wonderful light." [1 Peter 2: 9]*

## Offerings continually placed in the Inner Court:

• Shewbread – twelve unleavened cakes place on the table, also these were call the bread of presence. It represents the privilege of fellowship with God and the partaking of His word[19]. It was to be consumed by the priests privileged to represent the people and refreshed weekly.

---

[19] Cohen, Peter. 2012. *Messianic Good News*. October 4. Accessed May 1, 2015. http://www.messianicgoodnews.org/part-4-the-bread-of-the-presence/.

- Drink offerings – for the joy of fellowship with God and the joy at the completion of God's promises.
- Oil – olive oil, in this case the oil was used mainly for the light. This being only one of the spectrum of uses given this oil. It was to be fresh oil or that which was made from the first pressing of the first fruits of the olive tree. Additionally it was baked into the Shewbreads which were continually before Him.
- Incense – raising a sweet aroma before God the prescribed incense was frankincense

The first three of the offerings to be placed continually before God on the table of presence within the Inner Court of the Tent of Meeting. And they were the elements of a shared meal with God which was celebrated on a regular (weekly) basis with and before God. The drink and bread have carried over into the communion table we share with our God and our brothers and sisters. Often the oil that was found on the table of presence was considered a symbol of the pouring out of the Holy Spirit upon those who serve Him. So even down to today those serving as priests before God are asked to His Table to break bread and refresh our joy with Him.

## V. Outer Courtyard

Outer Court or Altar Court, was the place where public sacrifices and worship were conducted. It is where continual praises were offered, thanksgiving was brought, petitions were laid and forgiveness sought by the people were presented to the priesthood. This is the place where counsel was sought and commitments were made and thanks for blessing, provisions and protection are offered.

It is also where preparations were made by the priesthood for their intercessory approach before the Mercy Seat. It was here that the general Levites, servants of the Tabernacle or Temple and Hebrew worshippers stopped because of the intercession and intermediary requirements needed by the Holiness of God. This was where the High Priest who was designated in this position would prepare himself to then take the offerings and concerns of the people before the Mercy Seat in the Holy of Holies.

## Specifications:

- Surrounding the Tent of Meeting entirely and slightly lower in height than the Tent of Meeting.
- It's specification called for it to be twice as long as it was wide
- Entry was to be on the east end of the compound and to be 30 feet wide. This could be a representation of God's desire for our return for when we were expelled from Eden, Adam and Eve were sent to the east of Eden, so that on our return we would approach the eastern side of our original home.

## Adornments:

- Basin (Sea) – placed before the entrance to the Tent of Meeting so that all entering the tent could wash their hands and feet in purification prior to entering. It and the stand it was to be placed on were to be made of bronze.
- Brazen Altar of Burnt Offering was to be made of acacia wood overlaid with bronze. All of the utensils

used at the altar were also to be made of bronze. There were bronze horns at the four corners of the altar.

Now each of us that are called by His name have within us a place to bring our blessings, praises, thanks, petitions and confessions. We have our High Priest enthroned and the right hand of the Father so we now can enter boldly crying "Abba, Father". It is by renewing our minds and bodies with study and obedience that our preparations are done to receive His direction and counsel.

## Horns of the Altars:

In the context of the Tabernacle and Temple these horns were visual reminders of the royal power, dominion, glory, and fierceness of God. Both of the altars (Burnt Offering and Incense) were adorned with horns on all four corners. They [the horns] had the additional meaning as a visible symbol of sanctuary/salvation. This was where fugitives who could reach the altar of sacrifice and could cling to the horns of the altar to claim and obtain asylum. One of the Lord Jesus Christ's titles is the "horn of salvation".

*"He has raised up a horn of salvation for us in the house of his servant David" [Luke 1: 69]*

So like fugitives of the Old Testament, we can flee the penalties of our misdeeds. We have been given the gift of being able run to and cling to our "horn of salvation". This profound offer is the privilege of having a secure salvation and sanctuary we can hold on to with complete confidence.

## Court of the Gentiles:

The Court of the Gentiles was an addition made when the Temple replaced the Tabernacle as the central place of worship. It surrounded the Outer or Altar Court with covered colonnade porches. The space in its columns were used for teaching. This was where instruction, encouragement and conflict resolutions were conducted. It is the place where non-Hebrews were allowed to come to learn about God. This was to be the place where the curious could come to inquire about the things that made God's people so different from their surrounding world. It was in accordance with God's directions that the world was to find shelter and blessing within the "tent" of Israel. This Court reinforced the separatedness that was to be a characteristic of those who are called by His Name.

## Specifications:

- A colonnaded structure of porches that surrounded the Outer Court of the Temple
- It was visually open to the Outer Court so that what was conducted in the Outer Court was visible
- There was a warning barricade that prohibited foreigners from proceeding into the Temple precincts proper. It had tables for Temple business, and scribes.

# CHAPTER 8

## Old Covenant Conclusion

There was a time when the Tent of Meeting was outside of the camp of the Israelites. This was just before the actual construction of the Tabernacle given by God to Moses. It was a place outside of the camp where Moses could go to meet with and communicate with God. This was because when God called Moses up Mount Sinai to receive instruction the people became anxious and impatient. Then when the people felt Moses had been gone too long and they importuned Aaron to make them a physical idol to appeal to. This made the camp unfit for God to enter. He would not enter into the midst of the camp so polluted by idols, therefore He caused the place of meeting to be set up outside of the camp. Until such time as the camp was cleansed of the contamination of false worship God would not enter into their midst. We see in this our need to repent of our sin and cleanse ourselves before God before He will enter into our lives.

Then one more time God again elected to meet the needs of His people but went "outside the camp" to accomplish this. This was because the Temple where such sacrifices properly were to be made had become polluted in God's eyes. So, Jesus accomplished the perfect sacrifice of atonement and restitution for our sins outside of the "camp" aka city of Jerusalem. We should heed these occurrences as God has not changed his standards between then and now. God will not enter into our lives until we've made an effort to rid our tent of pollution by accepting the restitution and atonement made for our need and then trying to maintain it as fit place for Him to reside.

In preparing our Tabernacles we should consider the reminders contained in the colors, coverings and adornments of the original Tabernacle. From the colors, this should be a place that looks heavenward in truth and purity, cognizant of the royal sovereignty of God and riches found in Him, finally the sacrifice that has made it possible for our approach.

The coverings remind us of what we have received in the Lord; righteousness, the perfect sin offering, His standing substitute for our debts, and the covering of protection He offered us. His promised sovereign power to grant us sanctuary pictured by the horns on the altars. So within we can retreat to him in confidence and security and can go into His Houses with surety of surcease.

The adornments speak of the light that comes with the knowledge of God, the riches of His provision, and sanctuary we can find in abiding with Him. The external addition reminds us to be open to the curious and desirous who come to seek God.

Even the supports for the Tabernacle is indicative of God's purposes. The support wood acacia being so enduring and long lasting calls to mind God's enduring purposes. It calls to mind the foundational idea that God will overcome the most severe consequence of our disobedience death.

With the curtaining off of the various sections of the Tabernacle there was not only the sense of the restrictive honor of access, but also created a growing sense of intimacy as one progressed inward to the Holy of Holies. There was the publicly visible portion that gave evidence of the honor given to God. Then there was the inward portion of maintaining the light, joy, presence and aroma of blessings. As you entered the most closeted area there would be intimate and private communication with God.

This mixture of visible and intimate in three levels carries over into the New Covenant Church age. We have the internal space where the Holy Spirit resides with each believer to which we can repair seeking His counsel and comfort. Our bodies are analogous to the Inner Court of the Old Tabernacle as both Apostles Peter and Paul variously referred to our bodies as tents and temples. These tents/ temples are to first receive the fourfold covering from Christ. Then within we are to faithfully maintain the light of His Word, bring Him the sweet aroma of our offerings and share in the sustenance of His presence. They are where the decision to serve is confirmed. Then the churches are the visible manifesting of God before the world of our reverence, honor and service to God.

There is a richness in the studying of the Tabernacle/ Temple that only God could have given. For in it we find not only requirements and instructions for the journey of return we are on today; but others have shown that these structures contain hints of what that destination will be like.[20] In that it gives us pictures of the access requirements, the contents, and governing structure of God's Kingdom.

---

[20] Beale, G. K. 2004. *The Temple and the Church's Mission; a biblical theology of the dwelling place of God.* Downers Grove, Illinois: Intervarsity Press

# CHAPTER 9

———◆———

## New Testament Temple/Tabernacle

So now under the New Covenant – God's presence will come to be with and within every believer going with them daily as they journey through life once they have gone "outside the camp of the world" and cleansed themselves by repentance. As the next part of the journey commences we have the word given to us by Jesus:

> *"If you love me, keep my commands. And I will ask the Father, and he will give you another advocate to help you and be with you forever – the Spirit of truth. The world cannot accept him, because it neither sees him nor knows him. But you know him, for he lives with you and will be in you."*
> *[John 14: 15-17]*

So we have a constant companion as we walk on our journey to the home Christ has told us He is preparing for us. God sends the Holy Spirit once again to counsel and guide us. He enters into our tents. Just as the Israelites were to move when God moved and to rest or wait when He did not, so in our lives we are to follow His lead as He travels with and within us.

In many ways the physical specifications given the Hebrews for constructing the original Tabernacle could be figurative illustrations for our worship today. The Holy of Holies could be the seat of the Holy Spirit within the believer which we should keep clear of anything that absorbs our attention to the point of becoming an idol in our daily walk with God. The Inner Court of our tent of Meeting could be the believer himself where acts of worship are conducted continuously. The Outer Altar court of the Tabernacle and Court of the Gentiles, today would then become our physical church buildings where we go to bring our offerings and service, to receive the encouragement and corrections of fellowship, then to receive further instruction in God's ways, word, and worship. It is to be the place where the business of God's Kingdom goes forward. Lastly but not unimportantly, it should be a place where non-believers could come and be welcomed. They could come here to become acquainted with God that transforms his people in ways that are not known in the world and then to learn of His grace. As there is no longer a separation of Jew and Gentile under Christ, the Court of Gentiles should be incorporated into our churches to welcome all who come with good will.

That being so, now the soul, that void within each us, will again be filled with the resident it was designed for originally. And now it could be said to be our Holy of Holies, the place where God's presence resides. For that is where we believe the Holy Spirit takes up residence when the believer commits himself to serving God by accepting the gift of Grace made possible by Jesus Christ. Once filled when the Spirit comes to reside with the believer there is light that shines out from within each committed believer. For the Prophet Ezekiel recorded this promise in Ezekiel 37: 27;

*"My dwelling place will be with them; I will be
their God, and they will be my people."*

Some Bible translations translate 'dwelling place' as
Tabernacle. So with the indwelling of the Holy Spirit our
very own bodies would become a Tabernacle or Temple.
This is as the Apostle Paul has told us that our body is the
equivalent of the temple or tabernacle structure.

*"Do you not know that your bodies are temples
of the Holy Spirit, who is in you, whom you have
received from God? You are not your own; you
were bought at a price. Therefore honor God with
your bodies." [1 Corinthians 6: 19, 20]*

Therefore a Heart and Mind that are given to the worship,
study and service to God would stand as the Inner court of
our tabernacles. For that is where we bring our offerings of
our thoughts and efforts continually before Him and where
we strive to maintain His light in our lives by heeding His
word. In Philippians 4, Paul gives us guidance to help us
keep the impure and idols out of our tabernacle before God
for in verse 8 he tells us;

*"Finally, brothers and sisters, whatever is true,
whatever is noble, whatever is right, whatever is
pure, whatever is lovely, whatever is admirable –
if anything is excellent or praiseworthy – think
about such things."*

In this same manner what we call churches today would,
also, closely align with the Court of the Meeting/Gentiles. It
is where we come to enjoy the encouragement of fellowship
and gather under instruction in God's word, character,

promises and history. It functions to encourage believers in their walk and to reprove or correct errors. Perhaps more importantly it should be a place where seekers should feel welcomed so they can learn of God's love and grace.

In both instances of the Old Testament Tabernacle and Temple and the New Testament Temple and Tabernacle, God's presence could and would depart for a time when idols had been allowed to take up co-residence and pollute the tabernacle. These need not be material idols but they are anything which steals our primary focus from the giver of all righteousness, grace and provision. This is what God meant when He told us He was a jealous God, He has no inclination to share His worship and worshipers with another.

> *Be careful not to forget the covenant of the Lord your God that he made with you; do not make for yourselves an idol in the form of anything the Lord your God has forbidden. For the Lord your God is a consuming fire, a jealous God. After you have had children and grandchildren and have lived in the land a long time — if you then become corrupt and make any kind of idol, doing evil in the eyes of the Lord your God and arousing his anger, I call the heavens and the earth as witnesses against you this day that you will quickly perish from the land that you are crossing the Jordan to possess. You will not live there long but will certainly be destroyed. [Deuteronomy 4: 23 – 26]*

There are many instances in the Old Testament and one in the New Testament era when God withdrew from the Holy of Holies. Always God has given us warnings and cautions that we were going in the wrong direction before taking action. Then, if there were no course correction in the hearts of the people disastrous consequences followed. There are also times that there was a correction and the departure was forestalled. These corrections called for some very serious repentance and cleansing of the Temple, some might equate it to radical surgery. We have the warning that this can occur when we wander far from our first love, consider this from the letter to the Church at Ephesus found in Revelation.

> *"Yet I hold this against you: You have forsaken the love you had at first. Consider how far you have fallen! Repent and do the things you did at first. If you do not repent, I will come to you and remove your lampstand from its place." [Revelation 2: 4, 5]*

As the lampstand signifies both the light and the oneness we have in Christ; the admonishment that it could be removed is cautionary that we should tend to our source of light and love. Its removal would mean that His light had departed and that the unity with Him was broken. While we might still be going through the motions, we'd be without His approval, guidance and support. So as members in the Royal Priesthood we should examine what God expected of the appointed priests for the first Tabernacle.

## Priesthood:

Initially, the entire nation of Israel was to be God's representatives and ambassadors to the world. We find their commission in the words God had Moses speak to them as he, Moses, was preparing to go up onto Mount Sinai. These are the words spoken through Moses to Israel.

*"Now if you obey me fully and keep my covenant,
then out of all nations you will be my treasured
possession. Although the whole earth is mine, you
will be for me a kingdom of priests and a holy
nation.' These are the words you are to speak to
the Israelites."* [Exodus 19: 5-7]

While the nation as a whole was to continue as exemplars
before the gentile world, God states firmly that the whole
earth is His. Until humanity would be able to stand
individually in His, God's, presence Israel and now the
church were the portion to be set aside to act as intercessors
and intermediaries for the people in the Holy places.

These, priests, were the people who had the honor,
right and privilege to walk before God as exemplars for the
people and to serve at His altar and especially to have the
honor to enter before His Mercy Seat. Among the duties that
were assigned were tending to the upkeep of the Temple,
conducting the service and business of God's precincts,
instructing the people in God's ways; lastly and perhaps
most importantly guarding the holiness of the precincts.
Their portion was to be found in what was presented for
God's use and service. It was not to be found in the day-
to-day secular things. They were to be exemplars of the
goodness, provision, love and righteousness of God. They
stood intermediary and intercessors between the people
and God offering celebrations of grace shown, providence
given, and the surpassing goodness and greatness of God.
Then to proffer propitiation for trespasses and supplications
for the forgiveness concerning the sins of the past year. At
the Exodus, God directed that all the first born both man
and beast within the tribe of Israel were to be dedicated
to the service of God. Yet when the Tabernacle was being
established He selected out of all the tribes, one tribe to

stand in the stead for the "first born" males of the tribes. Thus the entire tribe was a substitutionary offering for the protection and salvation of Israel.

> *"Every firstborn male in Israel, whether human or animal, is mine. When I struck down all the firstborn in Egypt, I set them apart for myself. And I have taken the Levites in place of all the firstborn sons in Israel. From among all the Israelites, I have given the Levites as gifts to Aaron and his sons to do the work at the tent of meeting on behalf of the Israelites and to make atonement for them so that no plague will strike the Israelites when they go near the sanctuary." [Numbers 8: 17-19]*

This means under the old covenant structure the priesthood was a tribe that was set aside specifically by God to serve in this position. The tribe was set aside and hereditary. With the Advent of the Messiah, this was changed to being inclusive of all who named Christ as their salvation. No longer is the priesthood hereditary. No longer is a person selected to act as intermediary or intercessor for Christ has taken that position in perpetuity. We, as his royal priesthood, can go before the throne with confidence.

We have these verses confirming that upon accepting the Grace offered to us we become members of the set apart group of Royal Priests.

> *"Therefore, since we have a great high priest who has ascended into heaven, Jesus the Son of God, let us hold firmly to the faith we profess. For we do not have a high priest who is unable to empathize with our weaknesses, but we have one who has been tempted in every way, just as we are — yet*

*he did not sin. Let us then approach God's throne of grace with confidence, so that we may receive mercy and find grace to help us in our time of need."* [Hebrews 4: 14-16]

The priesthood we have joined and serve in is under a High Priest who knows the struggles we face by having faced them Himself yet won through in perfect obedience. We are reassured that our selection was not in error.

*"Who will bring any charge against those whom God has chosen? It is God who justifies. Who then is the one who condemns? No one. Christ Jesus who died — more than that, who was raised to life — is at the right hand of God and is also interceding for us."* [Romans 8: 33, 34]

Perhaps this was a fulfillment of one of the many prophesies found in Isaiah.

*I will set a sign among them, and I will send some of those who survive to the nations — to Tarshish, to the Libyans and Lydians (famous as archers), to Tubal and Greece, and to the distant islands that have not heard of my fame or seen my glory. They will proclaim my glory among the nations. And they will bring all your people, from all the nations, to my holy mountain in Jerusalem as an offering to the* LORD *— on horses, in chariots and wagons, and on mules and camels," says the* LORD. *"They will bring them, as the Israelites bring their grain offerings, to the temple of the* LORD *in ceremonially clean vessels. And I will select some*

*of them also to be priests and Levites," says the*
LORD. *[Isaiah 66: 19-21]*

This seems to bespeak of the Great Commission, the pouring out of the Holy Spirit at Pentacost, and the inclusion of gentiles in Temple service.

So can we continue living merely as laity presuming that others will perform the duties that have been placed before each of us? We each have a personal Tabernacle or Place of Meeting with God.

## Old Covenant – selected and hereditary:

When God called Israel out of Egypt, He claimed all of the firstborn of man and animal of Israel as His. Then at the giving of the Law and instructions for Tabernacle and Temple worship, He designated a substitutionary group that would stand for all of Israel. Instead of the first born male of every family from every tribe of Israel to serve God as revealed had been declared to Moses, the tribe of Levi now was set aside for God's service in Numbers chapter 8. In this action we see a substitutionary selection by God of the tribe of Levi to stand for the nation of Israel redeeming their sons and all her people. Thus this tribe was set aside unto God's service standing as substitute and intercessor the service that Jesus as Messiah would later stand for the world. These positions as designated by God were passed father to son through the ages so that even today there are Jewish surnames that are associated with priestly function.

# Duties:

Under the Levirate priesthood the various duties were divided among the various sons of Levi. So that you see the sons of Gershon, Kohath and Merari designated to serve the various needs of the Tabernacle. The sons of one [Gershon], whose descendant Aaron was, were set to serve at the altar, the High Priest was selected from among these. These were the ones who conducted the sacrifices and rites and rituals. The High Priestly position was the only one designated specifically to be permitted to enter the Holy of Holies. The sons of Kohath were tasked with providing music and maintaining the offerings and their vessels. The sons of Merari were tasked with the physical structures, their set up and take down and maintenance. These were also in charge of the gate keepers and wood gatherers who came from a gentile tribe that aligned with Israel by trickery as they entered the Promised Land. The entire tribe of Levi was to stand in the stead for the errors of the nation and the sons of Gershon were to stand as covering for errors committed by the Levites before God. The entire tribe was responsible for maintaining and guarding the holiness of God's house, mountain and people. They were to keep out of His presence any impurity and uncleanness.

So it is that the various families of the sons of Levi were arranged around the Tabernacle according to their duties as buffer for the people of Israel. In the specification of the various duties we see the tending and guarding responsibilities given originally in the Garden.

# Privilege:

The most evident privilege that the tribe of Levi had was that they were granted permission to approach the Mercy Seat in supplication and intercessory acts. They were given positions of example and power within the Nation to judge and pardon under God's supervision. They were looked to for guidance in God's desires and instruction. The least known privilege was that they were granted a portion of what was God's for their use. The priests from the sons of Aaron were, also, granted the right to eat of the Shewbread and drink of the wine that had been placed on the Table of Presence. This was done in the Inner Court or Holy Place weekly as fresh bread and wine were brought to be placed before God.[21]

# New Covenant – elected and individual:

Now by our electing to accept the new birth in Christ we have been elected to serve as God's exemplars before the world. Thus it is by individual choice that we have become members of the Royal Priesthood adopted into the Royal tribe. This privilege will no longer be passed automatically from parent to child, but must be individually chosen by conviction and consent. So it is our privilege to model for the next generation our obedience and joy in serving before our altar. So with the calling out of Israel God gave them the duties of being priests before the world, this calling was extended into the establishment of the New Covenant and the man chosen to lead was given to tell us what was to be our position.

---

[21] 1906. *SHOWBREAD*. Accessed May 2015. http://jewishencyclopedia. com/articles/13611-showbread.

*"But you are a chosen people, a royal priesthood, a holy nation, God's special possession, that you may declare the praises of him who called you out of darkness into his wonderful light." [1 Peter 2: 9]*

## Duties:

In fitting us to consider what would be our duties when we choose to walk before God. We each know we have been given gifts or talents, individually by our Creator which are to be used in service of God's purposes.

*"For just as each of us has one body with many members, and these members do not all have the same function, so in Christ we, though many, form one body, and each member belongs to all the others. We have different gifts, according to the grace given to each of us. If your gift is prophesying, then prophesy in accordance with your faith; if it is serving, then serve; if it is teaching, then teach; if it is to encourage, then give encouragement; if it is giving, then give generously; if it is to lead, do it diligently; if it is to show mercy, do it cheerfully." [Romans 12: 3-12]*

This is admittedly an incomplete listing of God given gifts. It is for each of us to discover our gift that has been given. A talent or passion we have that can be brought into His service are not only our gifts from God but are to be our gifts to God. Some are very visible such as teaching while others such as maintenance are not so visible except when not done, but are of equal value. So while the tasks are no longer divided by heritage they still need to be done. Within each of us under God's gifting and prompting we discover what gift He would have us bring to His service. Then it should be a love offering that we bring into His service.

In keeping with God being sovereign and having a plan for his creation, it would be reasonable to say as Mordecai did to Esther;

> *"For if you remain silent at this time, relief and deliverance for the Jews will arise from another place, but you and your father's family will perish. And who knows but that you have come to your royal position for such a time as this?"* [Esther 4: 14]

So, much as sometimes we might find things difficult and distressing something God has given us either as a talent or job was uniquely suited to the situation and needs around us. To shy away because we are not confident would be a shirking of God's intent and design for us; or worse yet a doubting of his wisdom and sovereignty. As we now are members of Christ's Royal priesthood, it behooves each of seek God's guidance and wisdom to discover what He has purposed for our service to be.

Yet perhaps our most vital duty remains guarding the precincts of our Tabernacle. That means keeping watch that unclean things do not enter in. And should they gain entrance root them out and cleanse the spot rigorously and thoroughly.

# Privilege:

Under the New Covenant, all who call on Christ have the freedom to approach the Father God crying "Abba" (daddy). No longer is the approach restricted to a privileged few who were the approved designated representative and that only after complex and lengthy ceremonial preparations on strictly circumscribed occasions. Indeed even after all that the approach was still a chancy proposition, in that death could result if all these things were not done correctly. Another great privilege is that with our adoption, we are joint heirs with Christ to the beauties of heaven.

> *"The Spirit himself testifies with our spirit that we are God's children. Now if we are children, then we are heirs — heirs of God and co-heirs with Christ, if indeed we share in his sufferings in order that we may also share in his glory." [Romans 8: 16, 17]*

Yet we are still bidden to come and partake of the bread and wine of the Lord's Table. As commemorative of the gift He has given to us.

> *"For I received from the Lord what I also passed on to you: The Lord Jesus, on the night he was betrayed, took bread, and when he had given thanks, he broke it and said, "This is my body, which is for you; do this in remembrance of me." In the same way, after supper he took the cup, saying, "This cup is the new covenant in my blood; do this, whenever you drink it, in remembrance of me." For whenever you eat this bread and drink this cup, you proclaim the Lord's death until he comes." [1 Corinthians 11: 23-26]*

## Priestly Preparation:

These preparations were to be done ritually every time it became a Levite's turn serve. They were meant to remind the Levite of the Holiness of God and the reverence with which he should regard the position he'd been designated to fill. The hazard here is that over time and repetition the symbolism can and often does become rote going through the motions without the deep emotional and spiritual examination they were to engender. There were three steps in proper preparation: cleansing, donning the vestments, and the anointing.

## Cleansing:

Washing was an important part of ritually consecrating the priests who would serve at the Altar. It had to be performed before receiving the anointing into the priesthood and again before performing the sacrifices for atonement. They had to be ritually clean before the consecration could go forward.

> *"Then bring Aaron and his sons to the entrance to the tent of meeting and wash them with water. Take the garments and dress Aaron with the tunic, the robe of the ephod, the ephod itself and the breast piece. Fasten the ephod on him by its skillfully woven waistband. Put the turban on his head and attach the sacred emblem to the turban. Take the anointing oil and anoint him by pouring it on his head. Bring his sons and dress them in tunics and fasten caps on them. Then tie sashes on Aaron and his sons. The priesthood is theirs by a lasting ordinance." [Exodus 29: 4-10]*

Under the Old Covenant before the priesthood could serve at the altar preparations started with ritual baths prior to donning the priestly garments. Even with the preparations done before dressing for service and receiving the anointing, when they were to proceed into the Inner Court, there were large basins placed before the stairs leading from the altar to the Inner Court, so that the priests could wash their hands and feet before approaching the inner precincts of the Temple.

On a non-priestly level one can see the need to conduct a thorough cleaning of our lives in the preparations that were in place to make one's home ready to properly celebrate the Passover. It always commenced with a thorough cleaning of the home. Specifically searching out yeast or leavening agents as the symbol of the sins that have entered over the year.

## Idols:

These idols could be physical or mental and needed to be regularly swept from our lives. In the Old Testament there were prescribed purification and rededication procedures to make the facility acceptable for God's purposes once again. First step was to physically remove and destroy the idol. Then the precincts are cleaned or washed. Then and only then could it be rededicated and purified. This has been a priestly duty since Adam, we are to guard and keep the sanctity and purity of our Temple.

Unfortunately idols creep into our Temple and need to be guarded against and regularly have to be rooted out. Israelites regularly were chastised for allowing idols not only into the Promised Land but also into the Temple itself by the various judges and prophets. There was even a time when this condition delayed God's entering into the lives of the Israelite camp. At that time, He had Moses set up the Tent of Meeting outside of camp because in their impatience for Moses' return from the mountain they had turn to idols.

> *"Then the Lord said to Moses, "Leave this place, you and the people you brought up out of Egypt, and go up to the land I promised on oath to Abraham, Isaac and Jacob, saying, 'I will give it to your descendants.' I will send an angel before you and drive out the Canaanites, Amorites, Hittites, Perizzites, Hivites and Jebusites. Go up to the land flowing with milk and honey. But I will not go with you, because you are a stiff-necked people and I might destroy you on the way." [Exodus 33: 1-3]*

These idols can be old things of comfort that call us back like the Egyptian golden calf. They can be items, ideas or relationships; things that grab our attention and fascinate us so much that they absorb all our thoughts and attention. The ones we most think of though, are material or monetary in nature. God will not share His precincts with idols. So it is that we must guard what we will allow into the precincts of God's Temple. God, still has no desire to share His space with idols and will withdraw His blessing and protection should idols be allowed to encroach into His places.

> *"They forsook all the commands of the Lord their God and made for themselves two idols cast in the shape of calves, and an Asherah pole. They bowed down to all the starry hosts, and they worshiped Baal. They sacrificed their sons and daughters in the fire. They practiced divination and sought omens and sold themselves to do evil in the eyes*

*of the Lord, arousing his anger. So the Lord was very angry with Israel and removed them from his presence. Only the tribe of Judah was left, and even Judah did not keep the commands of the Lord their God. They followed the practices Israel had introduced. Therefore the Lord rejected all the people of Israel; he afflicted them and gave them into the hands of plunderers, until he thrust them from his presence." [2 Kings 17: 16-20]*

So should we chance to emulate ancient Israel and forsake His ways, the Holy Spirit will again withdraw from us and let us go the ways of our own choosing.

## Vestments:

By definition these are the articles of ceremonial attire and insignia worn by ecclesiastical officiants and assistants as indicative of their rank and appropriate to the rite being celebrated. In the Old Testament, God gave very specific directions on how they were to be constructed and worn. They were symbolic of the reverence and awe expected when approaching God. They served, too, as reminders of the shortcomings we all are prone to. In the New Testament they are more internalized but should be kept in mind as we represent God to the world around us and equip us to confront the battle we will encounter. For now it is not by outward accoutrements that the world knows who serves but by the fruits produced. The main difference between the old and new covenant vestments is that under the old they were guards against ways man falls short of the glory and standards of God while the New are reminders of the strengths and grace that can be found in God.

## 1. Old Testament[22]

As the vestments were representational for the honor and beauty of God they must never be worn soiled stained or ripped. There were two sets of garments one (gold) for daily wear and the second (white) set aside specifically for the Day of Atonement. They consisted eight separate items to be worn. Each of the articles had a symbolic meaning to be considered as they were donned ceremonially prior to performing the priestly duties.

1. A tunic as a covering for the sin of killing.
2. Pants as a covering for impurity.
3. A turban as covering for the sin of pride.
4. A belt covering the heart as reminder of the need to control any improper thoughts.
5. The Breastplate was covering for errors made in judgement.
6. Ephod symbolized the need for atonement for idolatry.
7. A robe served as covering for evil speech.
8. Then a crown reminding the priest of the sin of arrogance.

## 2. New Testament

As Christ's Royal Priests, we, too, are to be fitted with the vestments of the whole Armor of God. These vestments are spiritual in nature and are visible only in the character and actions of the royal priesthood. They are to be donned each day as we walk before God as His representatives. The old vestments which were reminders of God's standards were no longer needed as Christ's sacrificial crucifixion had

---

[22] n.d. *Temple Institute The Priestly Garments*

completed the letter and intent of the Law. He has provided His new royal priesthood with all the covering required and if we keep before us the intent of His new vesture we recognize the debt of love that we hold. The listing of these vestments is found in Ephesians 6 verses 10 through 17.

1. Belt of Truth – belt connotes the general bond that holds all things together securely
2. Breastplate of Righteousness – protection of the heart wherein are precious gems of love and faith
3. Sandals of the Gospel – signifying a readiness to carry the Good News where ever and whenever it is needed.
4. Shield of Faith – symbolic of the protection from evils and false teaching and an object of trust
5. Helmet of Salvation – a helmet provides protection to the head, so our helmet of salvation provides us the protection of our hope in salvation against the doubts thrown up by the enemy.
6. Sword of the Spirit/Word of God – the symbol of the constant combat that truth has against false things.

It is a sobering contrast between the vestments for the priests of the Old and New Covenants. In one they wore reminders of how short humankind comes when measured against God's standards and requirements, this was while the only manner of approaching God was via perfect performance. In the latter, under the provisions of Grace, we are reminded of what God has done for us and His provisions for our protection. They, also, are preparations necessary for carrying God's love, word, salvation, and desire to a contentious world. From this change we should take encouragement and remember in joyous celebration what has been granted to us. This armor as our vestment prepares His priest/emissaries to go forward prepared truth and hope.

It is a wonder that God has taken contentious people from the point of striving against Him to the position of being capable of contending for Him with a rebellious world. At the time of God selecting a group to be His people, they took their national name from this forefather who had received his name from God after wrestling with God's angel.

> *"Then the man said, "Your name will no longer be Jacob, but Israel because you have struggled with God and with humans and have overcome."*
> *[Genesis 32: 28]*

To the point where we are now to strive against the unbelieving world and it's ruler for God's honor and glory.

> *"Dear friends, although I was very eager to write to you about the salvation we share, I felt compelled to write and urge you to contend for the faith that was once for all entrusted to God's holy people."*
> *[Jude 1: 3]*

## Anointing:

In the Old Covenant the priests received an anointing of oil poured out over them. Fresh pressed Olive oil formed the base of the Holy anointing oil which contained the finest sweet smelling spices [myrrh, cinnamon, fragrant can, cassia]. This oil was only to be used on that which was to be consecrated unto the Lord. It was not to be replicated for general use.

After the Old Testament priest had completed the ritual cleansing, purifications and vesting, then they would receive the symbolic anointing of an especially prepared oil that was poured over their head. This oil was symbolic of the anointing Holy Spirit that would inform and guide the priest in his duties as intermediary and intercessor between God and man. This can be seen as prefiguring the Holy Spirit being poured out and anointing followers of Christ when they accept His Lordship over their lives. It raises up a sweet aroma before God. It pictures the healing provided to our lives that is part and parcel in our reconciliation with God. Under the New Covenant anointing we are said to receive the anointing of the Holy Spirit and fire [or zeal] for God. As in the Old Testament, now in the New, it is the final step in priestly preparation for serving in the Tabernacle or Temple.

So as we repair to our Tabernacles we cleanse ourselves, to refresh our anointing with the Holy Spirit which has been poured out on us. We, then can don our armor to go out and face the world. We then can reflect and bring glory to our Lord God.

## Rites and Rituals:

These were actions that were proscribed to be performed at regular intervals or on special occasions. Many if not all were instituted by God in His instructions to Moses. The purpose or intent of making the people, priests and the place for meeting with God acceptable in God's eyes can be instructive for us in preparing our tabernacle to be suitable for God the Holy Spirit.

Most of these were instituted to keep before His people the fact that He had called them out as a separate people.

The one required of all Hebrews that set them apart from the surrounding populations was circumcision. This act was not immediately visible to others, but it was to be an awareness within every male Hebrew of their covenant with God as a separated and peculiar people unto God.

> *"Yet the Lord set his affection on your ancestors and loved them, and he chose you, their descendants, above all the nations — as it is today. Circumcise your hearts, therefore, and do not be stiff-necked any longer. For the Lord your God is God of gods and Lord of lords, the great God, mighty and awesome, who shows no partiality and accepts no bribes." [Deuteronomy 10: 15-17]*

This was then given elaboration by the writer of Romans with the explanation that the physical act was less important than the spiritual one of the heart.

> *"Circumcision has value if you observe the law, but if you break the law, you have become as though you had not been circumcised. So then, if those who are not circumcised keep the law's requirements, will they not be regarded as though they were circumcised? The one who is not circumcised physically and yet obeys the law will condemn you who, even though you have the written code and circumcision, are a lawbreaker. A person is not a Jew who is one only outwardly, nor is circumcision merely outward and physical. No, a person is a Jew who is one inwardly; and circumcision is circumcision of the heart, by the Spirit, not by the written code. Such a person's praise is not from other people, but from God." [Romans 2: 25-29]*

Circumcision was and is to be a rite of entrance into the separateness of God's people.

There were other rites of passage. Another was the presentation in Temple as dedication of the first born male to God. The next was the custom of standing before the people in either synagogue or Temple upon attaining to an age of responsibility. This was when a young man was considered mature enough to speak on matters of consequence. This rite of passage signified recognition of maturity and responsibility. Jesus participated in this rite as is seen in this episode.

> *"And when He was twelve years old, they went up to Jerusalem according to the custom of the feast. When they had finished the days, as they returned, the Boy Jesus lingered behind in Jerusalem. And Joseph and His mother did not know it; but supposing Him to have been in the company, they went a day's journey, and sought Him among their relatives and acquaintances. So when they did not find Him, they returned to Jerusalem, seeking Him. Now so it was that after three days they found Him in the temple, sitting in the midst of the teachers, both listening to them and asking them questions. And all who heard Him were astonished at His understanding and answers. So when they saw Him, they were amazed; and His mother said to Him, "Son, why have You done this to us? Look, Your father and I have sought You anxiously." And He said to them, "Why did you seek Me? Did you not know that I must be about My Father's business?" [Luke 2: 42-49]*

These and the rites of marriage and death, as well as those for health and hygiene were designed to keep His people prepared to be able to safely come into His Tabernacle and Temple.

Then there is the annual ritual every house in Israel would perform if they wished to participate in the celebration of the Passover. This was the rigorous cleansing of their homes of all yeasts.

> *"For seven days no yeast is to be found in your houses. And anyone, whether foreigner or native-born, who eats anything with yeast in it must be cut off from the community of Israel."* [Exodus 12: 18]

Yeast is considered symbolic of the effect that sin has on humanity. This is a reminder of how diligently those who would serve God should be trying to push sin out of our Tabernacles. As yeast is figurative of how a little bit of sin can change the character of the entire effort.

> *"Your boasting is not good. Don't you know that a little yeast leavens the whole batch of dough? Get rid of the old yeast, so that you may be a new unleavened batch — as you really are. For Christ, our Passover lamb, has been sacrificed."* [1 Corinthians 5: 6, 7]

## I. Sacrifice and Offerings under the Mosaic Covenant

Our modern understanding of the concept of sacrifice has wandered from the meaning that was ascribed to it in the Hebrew. Today we understand it as something that is given up or lost for a cause. But the word we translate as sacrifice has the connotation in Hebrew of "to come near, to approach; to become closely involved in a relationship with someone."[23] So in this way they can be adjustments we make to foster a relationship that is greatly desired.

Sacrifices are intended as a willing return of a portion of God's provision and gifts for God's use to His purposes. There are also sacrifices that are partial payment of restitution for debts and damages done during the year. The latter have been perfectly satisfied by Christ's perfect atoning sacrifice by his life and then death on the cross. These needed to be conducted to cover for mistakes that had been made. Sacrifices, also, were made in celebration of Thanksgiving. Petitions were accompanied by an offering sacrifice in hopes of favorable consideration.

> *"But who am I, and who are my people, that we should be able to give as generously as this? Everything comes from you, and we have given you only what comes from your hand. We are foreigners and strangers in your sight, as were all our ancestors. Our days on earth are like a shadow, without hope. Lord our God, all this abundance that we have provided for building you a temple for your Holy Name comes from your hand, and all of it belongs to you."* [1 Chronicles 29: 14-16]

These sacrifices and offerings consisted of either one or combination of an animal (meat and blood), grain (flour, unleavened or leavened), oil, wine or water. Our sin and trespass offerings and sacrifices have no value before God if they are not made with a heart of repentance. Without the

---

[23] January 24. Accessed May 5, 2015. http://www.mechon-mamre.org/jewfaq/qorbanot.hMamre, Mechon. 2012. *Qorbanot: Sacrifices and Offerings*. htm.

heart of repentance these offerings are only for show and therefore are hypocritical.

## Old Covenant [24]

Offerings and sacrifices, as established under the Mosaic Covenant were a provision in recognition that the Israelites would not be able to maintain the perfect performance throughout a single year. Therefore these sacrifices would be made and accepted as restitution payment for the past year's shortcomings. There were given specific requirements for each of the transgressions to be performed at regular intervals to cover the errors/sins committed in the past, these in no ways covered those that would occur in the future. There were also sacrifices of thanksgiving and blessing for recognition of those provisions and blessings that were received.

There was another side of these offerings and sacrifices, they spoke of the work of the Redeemer to come. They either spoke of what would be His works for God or of His works for mankind. On the works for God one offering pictures giving ones all to God, another pictures the purity of sinless life, the third looks to peace and sharing between God and mankind. These were the Sweet Savor offerings. The last two prescribed offerings shadow what the Redeemer would do for us. They were first to take away our sins and the last to atone for violations made against God's governance.

Each of the Sweet Savor sacrificial offerings would have three elements. These elements were blood or meat, grain or bread, and drink. The three Sweet Savor offerings were voluntary but the two Atoning Offerings were mandatory.

---

[24] 2015. *The Five Levitical Offerings.* Accessed 2015. http://www.bible-history.com/tabernacle/TAB4The_5_Levitical_Offerings.htm.

The last two would not include a drink offering as the joy of God's completed work was not being celebrated in them. The five sacrificial offerings are the Burnt offering, the Meal offering, the Peace offering, the sin offering and lastly the trespass offering. The two atonement offerings cover our errors of commission, omission and impatience. Impatience or presumption is covered in trespass which is our violation of God's sovereign rule. That is we presume to know His thoughts and timing, not seeking His guidance and consent. These are pictures of the complete work that the Messiah would accomplish.

## Types of offerings:

- Given totally: as in Burnt and Drink offerings to be either poured or burnt entirely before God.
- Shared between God and the approved representatives: as in Wave and Heave offerings that were lifted up to God and then portioned to the priesthood.

## Offering elements:

- Blood/Meat – the acceptable animals were bulls, lambs, goats and doves. All were to be male and without blemish.
- Grain/Meal – grain or flour unmixed with leavening agents or baked into an unleavened cake or bread. It was to be without yeast because yeast when it is present and allowed to grow changes the entire batch, much like sin when allowed to stand will eventually corrupt the entire.

- Drink – unadulterated or undiluted wine.
- Coin/Gems (silver or gold, jewels) – gifts of offering for the adornment, maintenance and the increase of God's House.

## Offering Occasions:

- Fellowship – an expression of God's desire and our desire to have a friendly companionship of shared interests. It was a shared meal between God and man.
- Peace – Rejoicing in the blessings of being at peace with God and man. It was a meal shared with the Lord. In this it closely aligns with the Church age's Communion Table.
- Recognition – occasions of honoring the Greatness, Goodness and Glory of God.
- Sin – acts of commission, omission or intent that violate the instructions and laws of God;
- Trespass – acts of presuming you know what God wants, of assuming you have His go ahead and you know how He will do these things, or being impatient and not waiting on His guidance and consent.

## Accepted Sacrifices and Offerings:

These consisted of animal, plant/vegetable and mineral return to God what He had provided to mankind. Some were given in rejoicing. Some were given in dedication. While others were in the sorrow of repentance, atonement and a small attempt at restitution. All were made as a visual and personal evidence of an earnestly desired forwarding of a relationship between both parties [God and man].

## 1. Animal:

These were generally bulls, sheep, goats or doves. These were all to be male and without blemish. In many cases the preferred were the first born animals. Some would consider this a foreshadowing of the Messiah being the first born son of God.

The blood or meat sacrifice was foundational and fundamental to the atoning restitution required for the sin debt that was owed. In the Bible it is recorded in the Laws that "In the blood there is life". This has been a proven statement of fact medically and figuratively.

> *"For the life of a creature is in the blood, and I have given it to you to make atonement for yourselves on the altar; it is the blood that makes atonement for one's life." [Leviticus 17: 11]*

We have a saying that something which is fundamental to a program or argument is "the meat of the matter". Thus the Old Testament animal sacrifices prefigured the fundamental cost that would be paid on the cross. These animals were either lambs, doves, goats or bulls that were only to be without spot or blemish. It told us that it would only be through the death and blood of the Lamb that we would receive life reconciled to God.

For with the establishment of Tabernacle worship it was blood that sealed the people to the covenant.

> *"Then he took the Book of the Covenant and read it to the people. They responded, "We will do everything the Lord has said; we will obey." Moses then took the blood, sprinkled it on the people and said, "This is the blood of the covenant that the*

> *Lord has made with you in accordance with all*
> *these words." [Exodus 24: 7, 8]*

For those who have entered into God's people under the New Covenant we have this assurance.

> *"In him we have redemption through his blood, the*
> *forgiveness of sins, in accordance with the riches*
> *of God's grace that he lavished on us. With all*
> *wisdom and understanding, he made known to*
> *us the mystery of his will according to his good*
> *pleasure, which he purposed in Christ," [Ephesians*
> *1: 7-9]*

This lasting sacrifice grants and seals the conditions and privileges of the Covenant and with the perfect fulfillment of the conditions of the sacrifice we no longer have to make annual atoning restitution via animal substitutes.

## 2. Plant:

Some plants referenced for worship and celebrations are grapes, olives, bitter herbs and grains. Grapes for the wine that celebrates the joy in God. Olives that serve purposes of light, healing and food. There is also a sense of permanence in the longevity of the olive tree. The bitter herbs are in remembrance of the experience of slavery.

### a. Grain/Meal:

"The Bread of Life" and Manna serve as major lessons in the value received in God's instruction. It represents both a Grace given and sustenance. In daily usage it connotes hospitality and acceptance. Expressed in the invitation to "come let us break bread together".

In the temptations of Jesus in the Wilderness, He rebuked Satan by saying;

*"Jesus answered, "It is written: 'Man shall not live on bread alone, but on every word that comes from the mouth of God.'" [Matthew 4: 4]*

Physical bread also serves as an object lesson of the benefits of cooperative community effort. Because to make bread, it is easier when we cooperate as a community providing differing talents and services towards a common goal.

Manna is a grace provided sustenance for life. It also gives us a picture of our need to refresh our supply from the source of life on a daily basis. As with Manna which melted and became unpalatable over time, the further along we go without returning to the freshness of the source the more it can become corrupted. It teaches that it should not be added to nor modified. For the more we modify, or add to it the less it gives of its original sweetness. We have the example in Exodus, when it was taken as it was given it was sweet as honey the more the Hebrews modified it the less palatable it became. It can also remind us how unusual grace can be in the world for the Hebrew meaning of the word Manna is "what is it".

Bread, a sustaining staple of life and one of Christ's names held prominent place in the Tabernacle and Temple. In the Holy of Holies some manna was placed in a jar kept in the Ark of the Covenant. This was a commemorative thanks offering for His provision sustaining the Israelites during the wilderness journey. In the Inner Court, twelve unleavened cakes (Shewbread or the bread of presence) were continually placed on tables within the sanctuary. This bread held significance that presaged the communion later share with Christ in the church. First it was to be continually on the table of presence picturing a continuous association. It was while on the table to be covered with frankincense that symbolizes the sweet aroma that our Savior has imparted to us by His obedience. It lastly was partaken by the serving priests within the Inner Court.

## b. Drink: [25]

The Drink offering was never offered alone after the giving of the Law. Under the Covenant Law it was only offered in conjunction with the "sweet savor offerings" and the wine was never adulterated or diluted. That is because the drink offering bespoke of the joy of God when a work in His plan reached a completion or when His people came into full possession of the blessings God designed for them. It was all given to God, none of it was to be consumed by the one making the offering. It was also, used at the completion of Nazirite vows. In the book of Leviticus, the drink offering is specifically mentioned in conjunction with three of the commanded Feasts. They are First Fruits (picturing the completed earthly mission and resurrection of Jesus), Weeks (picturing fulfillment of the promise of the giving of the Law and then the pouring out of the Holy Spirit upon His people) and Tabernacles (commemorating Israel being gathered into their homeland and prefiguring the final ingathering of His people). In fact there is only one reference to the drink offering before the giving of the law. That time, also, was the only time when this offering was offered without the accompanying meat and meal offerings.

[25] Langham, Andrew. 2006. "biblecentre.org/." "Topics/al_drink_offering.htm. Dec Friday 22.

That time it was an offering made by Jacob upon his return to Bethel.

*"Then God went up from him at the place where he had talked with him. Jacob set up a stone pillar at the place where God had talked with him, and he poured out a drink offering on it; he also poured oil on it. Jacob called the place where God had talked with him Bethel" [Genesis 35: 13-15]*

If the Drink Offering is symbolic of God's joy at completion of a portion or whole of His program, then we should examine the Apostle Paul's statement about being poured out as a drink offering. It was toward the end of his life of service and evangelism and he expressed the joy he had even in his trials at the glorious joy at serving God and seeing the growth of believers coming to know Him.

Two of the prophetic names for the Messiah are reflective of the intent behind the drink offering, "The Living Water" and the first fruit of the root of the vine of Jesse. In them there is a sense of anticipatory joy for the progress toward the restoration that God so desires to have with His creation. It is also recognition that drink is essential to life. For it is in God's Word that we can find life in abundance. In His word we find refreshment and the renewal. It is the very symbol of not only God's joy in our return but our joy in our returning to God's house. God has poured out himself not only in making full restitution for our debt but through His Word He has poured out His heart for us in one great love letter. This expresses His anticipated great joy at our return. We have been told that the return of just one to God causes rejoicing.

*"In the same way, I tell you, there is rejoicing in
the presence of the angels of God over one sinner
who repents." [Luke 15: 10]*

## 3. Mineral

At the start of Tabernacle/Temple worship these
consisted of gold, silver, bronze and gemstones. These were
dedicated to reflecting the glory of God. Most were used
in forwarding, constructing and appointing the structure
and those who would serve in it. These are specifically
mentioned as offerings brought to Moses to adorn the
Tabernacle of God and to robe the priesthood who would
serve for the people before the altars and in the Holy places.
So that these would be reflective of the richness and glory of
God. While today we don't tend to adorn our churches with
gold and gemstones, the coin that is offered is used to bring
the beauty and glory to the House of the Lord by adorning
it with obedience and love.

## VI. Sacrifices and Offerings under the New Covenant

As established by Jesus Christ at the last supper
[Passover] in what is now called Communion we have
representation of all of the three elements proscribed by
God with the giving of the law for appropriate "sweet savor"
offerings at the altar before the Mercy Seat. We have the
blood sacrifice that was given once for all in the crucifixion
of the only "lamb" that was absolutely without blemish. We
partake of the bread reaffirming our belief in and God's
desire for a renewed community of God and believers. The
wine carries recognitions of God's renewing refreshment

and sustaining of our life and our joy in God's continued presence. This wine is, also, symbolic of our recognition of God's joy at Christ's completed works. In its purpose it is to bring about the sharing or exchanging of intimate thoughts and feelings, especially the exchange on a deeply spiritual level.

Prayer is an offering we bring before the throne of God. We are bringing our praises and recognition of His greatness in love, provision and righteousness. We are bringing our sins and trespasses for his forgiveness and signifying our sorrow and repentance. We are bringing our desire for peace and fellowship and our joy that we are welcomed. We bring our concerns seeking His will. Lastly we acknowledge His sovereignty and our desire to abide in His kingdom. This is patterned in the prayer that should be the exemplar for all our prayer. We know it as the Lord's Prayer as it is the example Jesus taught to His disciples. From the Tyndale translation and as found in the Anglican Book of Common Prayer taken from Matthew chapter 6 verses 9 through 13[26].

> *Our Father who art in heaven,*
> *Hallowed be thy name.*
> *Thy kingdom come.*
> *Thy will be done on earth as it is in heaven.*
> *Give us this day our daily bread,*
> *And forgive us our trespasses,*
> *As we forgive*
> *Those who trespass against us,*
> *And lead us not into temptation,*
> *But deliver us from evil.*

---

[26] Orville Boyd Jenkins, Ed.D., Ph.D. 2007. *Reflections Debts or Tresspasses*. November 22.

*For thine is the kingdom, and the power,*
*And the glory, for ever and ever.*
*Amen.*

Our labor and the fruits of our labors are offerings we should lay before God. They are a portion of His provision for us on a daily basis that we turn back to Him as dedicated to His service. These should be the same as the offering of the first fruits requested in the Old Testament. These should be of our best efforts. As the writer of Romans stated nothing less than a total offering of our self is fitting gift to place on the altar of God.

> *"I beseech you therefore, brethren, by the mercies of God, that ye present your bodies a living sacrifice, holy, acceptable unto God, which is your reasonable service." [Romans 12: 1 (KJV)]*

This could be said in today's vernacular to describe one who is totally sold out to knowing and studying what pleases the one we love and worship. If we are sold out we are consumed with a desire to learn more and yet more about what pleases the object of our love. For how else can we do as Paul said in 2 Timothy 2: 15?

> *"Do your best to present yourself to God as one approved, a worker who does not need to be ashamed and who correctly handles the word of truth."*

## Priesthood Partaking

Under the priesthood established within the Mosaic Covenant the inheritance and portion was to be from

God. That meant a portion of what was brought to the Tabernacle and subsequently the Temple as offering and sacrifice to God was to be portioned out to the Levites. These were those offerings that were brought as wave or heave offerings, the portion that was to be for the priests was raised up before God signaling the willing offering of this to God's service.[27] A visible demonstration of God's provision for their well-being and service and a reminder of our complete dependence on God. Under the Tabernacle and Temple worship, there was one specified offering the Fellowship offering that was a shared meal. This meal was shared between the participants and God. It contained all three elements, meat, grain and/or vegetable, and drink. These offerings could be personal as in the completion of Nazirite vows, or they could be proscribed commemorative events such as Passover, Weeks and Tabernacles. Each time this meal was shared it was a visible reaffirmation of their covenant relationship. These offerings are also the ones that contained the element of drink signifying an occasion of joy.

Now per Christ's instruction we are instructed to partake in what was offered to God as the perfect sacrifice for our Salvation and Redemption. As there was no longer a need to perform a blood sacrifice for Christ made that sacrifice once for all and all time on the cross. To make further blood sacrifices would be tantamount to doubting the sufficiency of God's provision again.

> "He did not enter by means of the blood of goats and calves; but he entered the Most Holy Place once for all by his own blood, thus obtaining eternal redemption." [Hebrews 9:12]

[27] Elwell, Walter A. 1997. *Offerings and Sacrifices.* Accessed May 1, 2015. http://www.biblestudytools.com/dictionaries/bakers-evangelical-dictionary/offerings-and-sacrifices.html.

When we partake of the Communion table, we commemorate this act for our salvation and partake in the bread and drink celebrating a renewal and reaffirmation of the community both God and we desire here on earth with us and eagerly anticipating the joy of the return of the King of Kings. It is a celebration of God's joy at the completion of Christ's coming and our acceptance and embracing of it meaning and purpose. It is a visible reaffirmation of our Covenant relationship with God and our promise to hold to it.

## VII. Feasts & Festivals

While today there are many commemorative feasts, festivals and celebrations within the Hebrew calendar, there are only seven that were instituted by God when He gathered His people to establish them in their home. These were given at the same time as He gave us the Commandments and Laws. They were part of the cycle of worship and remembrance begun with the construction of the Tabernacle. Passover and the feast of Unleavened Bread were established prior to the departure from Egypt [Exodus 12], in Exodus 23 God established the celebrations of First Fruits and Ingathering. In Leviticus, the Day of Atonement (16) is added to the list.

They are in order by season: [28]

Spring (the time of year symbolic with the beginning of new life)

1. **Passover** – Celebration of God's Forgiveness, Grace and Redemption. This was a concrete picture of the first requirement for a return to God, manumission

---

[28] n.d. *Orah Sheb Yshua.*

from enslavement. He freed his chosen ones physically from bondage, now we equate this to the sacrifice of our Messiah for our freedom from the bondage of sin.

2. **Unleavened Bread** – Symbolic celebration of the need and the desire to eliminate sin. It is a preparation of the ground in our lives to receive the gift of salvation anticipating the indwelling Holy Spirit.

3. **First Fruits** – Celebration of the provisions of God (has been associated with the resurrection as the first fruit of God's harvest). With the resurrection of Jesus giving new meaning of the first fruit of Salvation.

Mid-year (the time of year when the first evidence of the harvest to come is visible; it is also a time of tending to the crop so that it develops to its fullness)

4. **Weeks** – Receiving of the Law given approximately 120 days after Israel left Egypt and in the 50th week after Israel was redeemed from physical slavery. A picture of the redemption from a spiritual slavery to idolatry and immorality. During the Church age we celebrate this as Pentacost as during the Feast of Weeks it was that the promise of the pouring out of the Holy Spirit upon believers was fulfilled.

Fall (culminating in the Harvest)

5. **Trumpets** – Redemption/Restoration the association here is to the Sabbatical and Jubilee years which were announced with the sounding of trumpets. These were designated times of return, when the people were given pardon, freedom from debt and slavery, then returned to a right standing within

the community of Israel. This was to be announced throughout the land by the blowing of trumpets.

There will be one more blowing of the Trumpets of God throughout the world at the end of times;

*"In a flash, in the twinkling of an eye, at the last trumpet. For the trumpet will sound, the dead will be raised imperishable, and we will be changed. For the perishable must clothe itself with the imperishable, and the mortal with immortality"* [1 Corinthians 15: 52, 53]

6. **Atonement** – Propitiation/Reconciliation these were acts to be performed annually to make small payment on the debt that had accumulated over the preceding year. With the perfect sacrifice of the Lamb of God that made atonement once for all, no longer are the sacrifice of animals required, but repentance is the expected atonement for recognized debts incurred.

*"He is the atoning sacrifice for our sins, and not only for ours but also for the sins of the whole world"* [1 John 2: 2]

7. **Tabernacles** – a commemoration of God's dwelling with His people on their journey to the home God had prepared for them [Israel]. It pictures His promise to be with us on our journey and that God has every intent to gather His people to Him. Celebrates a thanksgiving for His provision. We commemorate the time that caused Moses to sing:

*"In your unfailing love you will lead the people you have redeemed. In your strength you will guide them to your holy dwelling." [Exodus 15: 13]*

In addition we have not only the Marriage Feast of the Lamb, but also the celebration that is anticipated at the culmination of our journey of ingathering when God will dwell with His own.

*"And I heard a loud voice from the throne saying, "Look! God's dwelling place is now among the people, and he will dwell with them. They will be his people, and God himself will be with them and be their God." [Revelation 21: 3]*

So even in the Feasts and Festivals God instituted for His people, we can see the pattern and plan that God had set in motion to accomplish our redemption, salvation and ultimate restoration. In the yearly cycle the structure of God's intent and desire for a reconciliation and restoration with us can be understood and anticipated. With the Advent and Resurrection of Jesus Christ, we can see the fulfillment of several of the God given promises contained in these proscribed feasts and festivals. We have additional reason to celebrate these promises as confirmation of God's constant love and have faith in His promised provision. The fulfillment gives us confidence in the remaining promised portions that bring us to our joyous reunion in the New Heavens and Earth[29].

In the modern church liturgical calendar, which oddly enough is somewhat like the Hebrew religious calendar in that it does not coincide with the secular calendars. In

---

[29] n.d. *Biblestudytools.org.* bakers evangelical dictionary feasts and festivals of israel

our feasts and seasons we continue to celebrate the love, guidance and providences of God. But not necessarily in the old Hebrew order of celebration. Starting with Advent we see the meaning of the saying "from the womb of a woman will come the light of the world". The two calendars are similar in that the "new year" does not align with the secularly designated New Year's Day. Both religious calendars start anew after the celebrations of Thanksgiving.

## Church Calendar Year:

1. **Advent** – A commemoration of God's fulfillment of His promise to send us the Kinsman-Redeemer, Savior and Messiah.
2. **Christmas** – The culmination of the Advent Season, the coming of the perfect Lamb and Messiah as a humble servant.
3. **Epiphany** – this is most frequently associated with the coming of Magi to worship the Messiah. However the dictionary meaning of an illuminating discovery, a realization, or disclosure is apropos during this time; in that we reflect on the revelation of God's plan of salvation.
4. **Lent** – our expression of a desire to deny sin. It is a recognition of God's intent to call us out of the world and to separate us as His own.
5. **Holy Week** – the culmination of God's second Passover. Like Passover this is a stepped commemoration of what God performed to bring us out of bondage.
6. **Easter** – Redemption fulfilled and Reconciliation process initiated.

7. **Pentecost** – God's promise of a Comforter and Advocate with the indwelling of the Holy Spirit (50 days after the Resurrection) to walk along with us daily.

8. **Thanksgiving** – Celebration of not only the provision for our daily needs but also His provision of Grace. It, also, should cause us to remember the promised joy of the reunion to come.

The Old Testament festival feast of Tabernacles most closely aligns with our modern celebration of Thanksgiving. Both are celebrations of God's provision and the ingathering of the harvest. Both are celebrated in the same portion of the calendar year. Both end the liturgical calendar year. In some ways one can say Tabernacles is the commemoration of the time God gathered in the harvest of His people into the land He had prepared, Israel.

> *"Go and proclaim in the hearing of Jerusalem: 'This is what the Lord says: 'I remember the devotion of your youth, how as a bride you loved me and followed me through the wilderness, through a land not sown. Israel was holy to the Lord, the first fruits of his harvest; all who devoured her were held guilty, and disaster overtook them,' declares the Lord."* [Jeremiah 2: 2, 3]

So today we can say that God is again preparing to gather in a harvest and bring His people into the home He has made for them. He is gathering to Himself all those who are called by His name. Winnowing them out of the fields of the world and into His house those who hear and accept Him. We are again setting out on a journey of following

Him as His bride as He is ingathering us through another wilderness journey to the Home He has prepared.

> *"When he saw the crowds, he had compassion on them, because they were harassed and helpless, like sheep without a shepherd. Then he said to his disciples, "The harvest is plentiful but the workers are few. Ask the Lord of the harvest, therefore, to send out workers into his harvest field." [Matthew 9: 36-38]*

God has set us on the path towards home, and He is gathering all who choose to Him. His people are invited, no instructed, to be helping in this ingathering.

# CHAPTER 10

~~~~~~~~~~

## Obligations

Most of us hear the word obligation and think of a debt owed, while there is that aspect to our relationship with God there is also the sense of commitment to a course of action upon making a vow. With God there are elements of both meanings to the word, we are eternally in debt to Him for the Grace He has provided for our salvation. When we enter into the covenant relationship via our declarations of repentance and baptism, we have given our vows to God that we will follow Him and study to please Him. In other words we say that we wish, desire and commit ourselves to being his disciple and abiding by his covenant rules. This is essentially our obligating ourselves to the terms and conditions of this covenant. Our obligation takes shape in our increasing awareness of the character of God and his standards. This in no way expects perfection in our performance and adherence to these standards. But it does imply our desire to become more like Him and our continuing attempts at improvements. It can start with merely the respect we show the vessels and structures that have been dedicated to His service, our bodies. Ultimately it means obedience to His sovereignty and governance in our lives and world.

Without a good understanding and awareness of God's character and standards we cannot fulfill the position God has placed us in. That is the position of being His exemplars before the world. This position is twofold. The first is to be an attractive exemplar of the joy and benefit of living by His standards, so that those around us wish to know what it is that we have. By demonstrating what God provides for His people in changed lives, peace that "passes understanding, and a love that exceeds what the world knows; we show the loving God who yearns for His creation. The second purpose or position we are to fulfill is contained in what we know as the 'Great Commission'. It was given to the disciples after they had signaled their willing obedience by going into Galilee as He instructed them after the resurrection.

> *"Then Jesus came to them and said, "All authority in heaven and on earth has been given to me. Therefore go and make disciples of all nations, baptizing them in the name of the Father and of the Son and of the Holy Spirit, and teaching them to obey everything I have commanded you. And surely I am with you always, to the very end of the age." [Matthew 28: 18-20]*

This then would be a fulfilling of the prophecy contained in Noah's blessing of his son's Shem and Japheth. It was also alluded to by the Prophet Isaiah who foresaw the sending out to the world of God's invitation and word.

> *"Praise be to the Lord, the God of Shem! May Canaan be the servant of Shem? May God extend Japheth's territory; may Japheth live in the tents of*

Shem, and may Canaan be the servant of Japheth."
[Genesis 9: 26, 27 (KJV)]

From Shem descended the peoples known as Semites of whom Israelites are one group. Genealogically much of the gentile world is traced through the descendants of Japheth. While the third son of Noah is not mentioned, it is only one of that son's children that receives opprobrium. That son, Ham, had three other sons who were not included in the curse placed on Canaan and his descendants.

In order to perform these obligations we need at a bare minimum to maintain the vessels of worship and service. As our bodies are considered to be the temple where the Holy Spirit resides with us. We would be wise to guard against idols gaining entrance into the precincts of our temples. Then we should strive to keep the source of our light refreshed and well supplied. For if we desire the indwelling Holy Spirit to be with us we should keep the place of His residence pleasing to Him.

Idols come at us in many forms and tempting appearances. They need not be physical to become something that consumes the heart and mind to the detriment of attending to the one who truly loves us and yearns for our attention. So it takes one who is on guard continuously to discern the gradual sliding towards idols to keep them from polluting the precincts of the Holy Spirit. For if these places become polluted God has in the past and will do so now; withdraw from the proximity of impurity.

## I. Keeping oil for the lamps

This is a primary duty, as not only are we to be watchful for the bridegroom's return, but also, it means maintaining a vessel properly filled with the Holy Spirit. For without the light provided by the Holy Spirit we would be in the dark about the days and times that Jesus told us to be cognizant of and to understand. This is the light that illumines our understanding of God. As His betrothed, we are to be watchful for His return. Likewise as we are His servants we are to guard our Lord's possessions.

> *"Be on guard! Be alert! You do not know when that time will come. It's like a man going away: He leaves his house and puts his servants in charge, each with their assigned task, and tells the one at the door to keep watch. Therefore keep watch because you do not know when the owner of the house will come back — whether in the evening, or at midnight, or when the rooster crows, or at dawn." [Mark 13: 33-35]*

We can see this coming only if we have our lamps lit and shining. Only when we are awake, aware and have the light to see our way, can we be fully prepared for understanding the times in which we are living. It is expected that we are to prepare the way for His arrival. It is, also, expected that we can properly explain His honors and riches so that others might also desire Him.

> *"And do this, understanding the present time: The hour has already come for you to wake up from your slumber, because our salvation is nearer now than when we first believed. The night is nearly over; the day is almost here. So let us put aside the deeds of darkness and put on the armor of light." [Romans 13: 11, 12]*

With this light we are better fitted to be obedient to His sovereignty. For not only is the Word "a lamp unto our feet" so that we might not stumble it is to shine before the darkened world. This light will aid in our desire to bring others of the world to a saving knowledge of God for as our light shines in our lives it attracts the attention of those around us opening the way to share with them the joy of our Lord.

## II. Obedience

We pledged our obedience when we first accepted the Grace of God's forgiveness. The first step in our obedience is to make ourselves available for His direction, teaching and discipline. As we enter into our Tabernacles we should come with having read for understanding His word then willingly listen for His guidance to aid our comprehension. Then we should be prepared to signal our obedience by stepping out in faith where He leads even when we don't see the entire road ahead. Then comes perhaps the hardest form of obedience, waiting on His time.

In Proverbs we find this instruction:

> *"Listen to my instruction and be wise; do not disregard it. Blessed are those who listen to me, watching daily at my doors, waiting at my doorway. For those who find me find life and receive favor from the Lord." [Proverbs 8: 33-35]*

This gives us the sequence of obedience which leads to wisdom. That is: listen to God's instruction, watching or examining and observing, then waiting. If we follow this we have the promises of God's favor, wisdom and life.

Susan E. Craig

## III. Listening

In this day and age, many is the time we do not listen for understanding but for response. That is we are thinking of what we will say, not about exactly what is being imparted to us. But unless we can calm our minds for listening to comprehend what we are hearing and not thinking about what we will be saying in response or argument we will miss much of what God has for us. It is from our study that we can listen in our hearts and minds open to the promptings of the Holy Spirit. It is then that we become coachable and able to learn of our God.

Much of the frenetic sounds that we continually have around us appears to possibly be a wall to keep at bay what we fear we might find in the silence that allows the still small voice to speak to our hearts. Do we doubt that God wants nothing but the best for us? Or do we wish not to hear the instructions given? Or yet again do we wish to avoid the tests designed to refine us for they can be painful?

Do we look for the grandiose announcements and the spectacular shows? Yes God can use those to get our attention, but most often it is in gentle instructions that He speaks to his disciples. It has been that way since Eden when He walked with Adam in the cool of the evening. Elijah recorded his experience in listening for the Lord in 1 Kings. In this passage Elijah demonstrates expecting the loud and spectacular but finding God in the gentle quiet.

> The Lord said, "Go out and stand on the mountain in the presence of the Lord, for the Lord is about to pass by." Then a great and powerful wind tore the mountains apart and shattered the rocks before the Lord, but the Lord was not in the wind. After the wind there was an earthquake, but the Lord was

140

*not in the earthquake. After the earthquake came
a fire, but the Lord was not in the fire. And after
the fire came a gentle whisper. [1 Kings 19: 11, 12]*

It was in this stillness that King David was instructed
to be still and know [Psalm 46:10]. We should heed this
instruction and still our activities and quiet ourselves to
hear what we need to learn.

## IV. Study

We have a multitude of reasons to study God's Word.
The primary reason is that is the best way for us to get to
know our beloved to the intimate level of relationship He
desires for us. Then it is, when understood and practiced, a
most excellent guide for our lives, in essence it is the owner's
manual for life. Then our understanding and adherence to
its precepts will make us fit to fulfill the purpose for which
we were designed. Lastly, but in no ways unimportant, it
will guard us from being led astray by plausible arguments
and teachings that abound in the world.

In Hebrew when God says He wishes to know His
people (as He does throughout the Bible) it is said using the
same Hebrew word for knowing as was used for the joining
of Adam and Eve [Genesis 4: 1]. He wishes for His Bride to
know Him as thoroughly as He knows her. In our daily
walk, and our daily dealings we find the Bible's instructions
are most certainly as the Psalmist said in Psalms 119:

*"Your word is a lamp for my feet, a light on my
path." [Psalms 119: 105]*

Also, in the Old Testament, when it was God's purpose to return Israel from Babylon, His chosen leader was Ezra. We learn from this choice that God selected one who had studied and learned God's ways and one who had purposed to share this knowledge.

> *"He had begun his journey from Babylon on the first day of the first month, and he arrived in Jerusalem on the first day of the fifth month, for the gracious hand of his God was on him. For Ezra had devoted himself to the study and observance of the Law of the Lord, and to teaching its decrees and laws in Israel." [Ezra 7: 9, 10]*

Thus we see that Ezra had made himself fit for doing God's will and purposes before God set him to the task. Then in the New Testament, the Bereans are held up for their practices for us to emulate today.

> *"Now the Berean Jews were of more noble character than those in Thessalonica, for they received the message with great eagerness and examined the Scriptures every day to see if what Paul said was true." [Acts 17: 11]*

If even the words of the Apostle Paul were to be held up against the Word of God, how much more so should God's people be following this example, so as not to be lead astray by high sounding pronouncements?

# Reading:

This is not only reading the Bible, although it is the primary source of instruction. We, also, have the study and writings of Godly men and women who have gone before us. It is by comparing and questioning that we, when we are quiet under the instruction of the Holy Spirit that the light grows stronger in our lives. It is amazing the depth of meaning that can be found on the pages of the Bible. It has been proven that these depths cannot be seen in a single cursory reading. God through the Holy Spirit continually brings out ideas and concepts that are cogent to the time and conditions of each reading. Each one of us has a responsibility to question for understanding to see that what our teachers are telling us aligns with God's given Word. It is essential that these teachings align with what God has said in His Word for it is as easy now as it was then to go along with what we wish to hear and not with what we need to hear. It is very easy to think that others are more knowledgeable or more experienced than ourselves and take without question their pronouncements even though they are as human as we are and just as capable of going astray. Then there will always be those of the deceiver who will try to bend God's words to their own purposes.

*"But there were also false prophets among the people, just as there will be false teachers among you. They will secretly introduce destructive heresies, even denying the sovereign Lord who bought them — bringing swift destruction on themselves. Many will follow their depraved conduct and will bring the way of truth into disrepute. In their greed these teachers will exploit you with fabricated stories. Their condemnation*

*has long been hanging over them, and their destruction has not been sleeping." [2 Peter 2: 1-3]*

So it lies with each believer to be familiar with the Word as God has given it to us.

## Application:

James in his epistle gives us the warning that it is all well and good to listen to the word and to know it by study but we fool ourselves if we think that that is all that is asked of us.

> *Do not merely listen to the word, and so deceive yourselves. Do what it says. Anyone who listens to the word but does not do what it says is like someone who looks at his face in a mirror and, after looking at himself, goes away and immediately forgets what he looks like. But whoever looks intently into the perfect law that gives freedom, and continues in it — not forgetting what they have heard, but doing it — they will be blessed in what they do. [James 1: 22-25]*

It is only in practicing or applying what we have understood that it becomes a part of who we are and what we are to become. It is also in practice where we most often find the gaps in our understanding. It often sends us back to the teacher of our souls for correction and explanation. It has been shown that it takes at least forty days of consistent practice for a new form of behavior to become second nature and an integral part of one's nature. Application is the way we signal that we have understood and incorporated what lessons have been taught. In the words of the Apostle Paul to Timothy, we are to by our applying what we have read and heard:

> *"Do your best to present yourself to God as one approved, a worker who does not need to be ashamed and who correctly handles the word of truth." [2 Timothy 2: 15]*

If we could understand perfectly the first time, if we could perform perfectly, practice and repetition would not be the norm for us in conforming to what God asks of us.

The world makes its judgements and assumptions about our beloved by comparing our words and our actions to see how well they match up. So when our words and actions do not match we detract from the glory due God. When others can see how God's instruction and guidance looks in practice it opens opportunities to share our joy and contentment with others.

## Sharing:

As we share and explain what we have discovered we gain a greater grasp of the lesson(s) that was placed before us. The flip side of this is that the questions and experiences of another who we share with can lead to our own deeper understanding of the concepts and precepts that we are learning in our journey to become like Christ. It is pleasing to God for us to share all things with our brothers and sisters and to bear them up for it shows us to be His disciples.

> *And do not forget to do good and to share with others, for with such sacrifices God is pleased. [Hebrews 13: 16]*

## V. Taking the first step

Sometimes God asks us to take the step of faith. This usually means acting on His word without our completely understanding the why's and where for's of the leading. But taking this step is the opening that allows God's blessing to flow to and through you. It is the way we answer His questions "do you love Me?"; "do you truly desire to know Me?" and "Will you walk before Me?" For each of us are being asked like the Apostle Peter;

> *"The third time he said to him, "Simon son of John, do you love me?" Peter was hurt because Jesus asked him the third time, "Do you love me?" He said, "Lord, you know all things; you know that I love you." Jesus said, "Feed my sheep." [John 21: 17]*

So then it is that we demonstrate our love, desire trust, and willingness by stepping out in faith even when we do not totally understand. This trusting in His love and concern for our well-being raises a sweet aroma before the throne of God.

Sometimes as with Abraham we are asked to signify our willingness to sacrifice something that is very dear to us. For God desires the demonstration of our complete love, trust and obedience, as when God called Abraham to sacrifice his son. Once the demonstration was made:

*"Do not lay a hand on the boy," he said. "Do not do anything to him. Now I know that you fear God, because you have not withheld from me your son, your only son." [Genesis 22: 12]*

As with Abraham once we have shown our compliance and obedience, we open ourselves to the fullness of God's promises and blessings. For it was only after Abraham demonstrated his willingness to give back as sacrificial offering, the son of his heart that the march toward the building of the nation that is Israel began.

God desires to see demonstrated our love and desire to honor His name by offering not only our best but our all.

## VI. Waiting

Perhaps the hardest thing for human beings to model is the fruit of patience. But we presume on God's sovereignty when we rush ahead of Him in doing things. This is the cause of many stumbling failures. For when we rush ahead of God after we are told to wait on the Lord's go ahead before we can proceed we tend to barge in before all is in readiness. When we impatiently rush ahead often we later find that the full benefit that God intended is thwarted and sometimes it actually can be counterproductive to God's glory. If we grasp hold of the confidence that God's ways and timing brings about the best results.

*"I remain confident of this: I will see the goodness of the Lord in the land of the living. Wait for the Lord; be strong and take heart and wait for the Lord." [Psalms 27: 13, 14]*

This confidence is available to all of God's obedient children for God has promised us his love, providence, and strength. So we, as impatient as we can become, must learn that the best way is for us to wait upon the Lord. The exiles in Babylon would surely have liked to act on their own to take God's promise of return in their own time, but they were counseled by God through Jeremiah:

> *"This is what the Lord says: "When seventy years are completed for Babylon, I will come to you and fulfill my good promise to bring you back to this place. For I know the plans I have for you," declares the Lord, "plans to prosper you and not to harm you, plans to give you hope and a future. Then you will call on me and come and pray to me, and I will listen to you." [Jeremiah 29: 10-12]*

They waited and did not take their return into their own timing which would have been in defiance of the Babylonian ruler. In the end, they obtained the permission of the Babylonian ruler to return and reconstruct. This return is documented in the Books of Ezra and Nehemiah.

As the Lord, God is faithful and true to his word we have many reasons to not take matters into our own hands to bring about the desired end. He has given us counsel to patiently wait on Him at regular intervals as a caution to marching to our own timing because the end results when we wait are so much more than we envisioned in our own capacity. Too many times throughout history God has demonstrated to us that indeed His ways and thoughts are not as ours in that His plans have been accomplished in manners that do not conform to our sensibilities and methods.

*"Then the Lord replied: 'Write down the revelation and make it plain on tablets so that a herald may run with it. For the revelation awaits an appointed time; it speaks of the end and will not prove false. Though it linger, wait for it; it will certainly come and will not delay.'" [Habakkuk 2: 2, 3]*

So we are to wait on the Lord's timing and guidance in forwarding His revelation. But during this wait we are to keep God's plans fresh in our minds and to make all aware of the coming events.

## Betrothed:

The Church is referred to as the 'bride of Christ'. John the Baptist and Jesus both referred to Jesus as the bridegroom.

*"Jesus answered, "How can the guests of the bridegroom fast while he is with them? They cannot, so long as they have him with them." [Mark 2: 19]*

And then John the Baptist in calling himself the friend of the bridegroom said of Jesus:

*"You yourselves can testify that I said, 'I am not the Messiah but am sent ahead of him.' The bride belongs to the bridegroom. The friend who attends the bridegroom waits and listens for him, and is full of joy when he hears the bridegroom's voice. That joy is mine, and it is now complete. He must become greater; I must become less." [John 3: 28-30]*

That being so, we should again look at the Covenant Marriage to see the intent, conditions and relationship it pictures. In the symbol of this Covenant are the elements of its intent: a totality, wholeness, original perfection, the self, the infinite, eternity, and timelessness. Then perhaps consider the Church Age as our betrothal period, which by custom is the waiting period during which the betrothed prepare themselves for their impending union. They are to use this time to become more deeply acquainted with the person and character of their espoused mate. This is only achieved by studying the likes, dislikes and character. We should seek to be ready to answer such questions as those that were posed by the friends of the beloved in Song of Solomon. In Song of Songs 5: 9-10 they ask;

> *"How is your beloved better than others most beautiful of women? How is your beloved better than others, that you so charge us?"*

This evidence of becoming like one another is the result of careful and constant study. So that the answers come immediately to our lips when asked. As we seek the pleasure and glory of the beloved. Each partner showering love and joy and adoration onto the other. This by serving one another, seeking one another's glory. This should be our constant preparations for becoming a fitting bride to enter into the Marriage Feast.

Hebrew betrothal tradition had two times that the bride signified her willingness to accept her intended. Both used wine to signal her readiness. The first time came after serving all but herself with a glass of wine, she listened to the qualifications of the suitor and if her father agreed to the offer; then and only then if she chose would she pour herself a cup of wine and take a sip. Then the bridegroom would propose directly to her. He would consecrate himself to her in righteousness, in judgement, in loving kindness, in mercy and faithfulness. Then he would pour out a cup of wine and offer it to her. If she accepted the cup and drank of it the covenant was sealed. Then the man promised on oath to return for the young woman when all the wedding preparations were complete. She remained with her parents maintaining a constant preparedness for the wedding date would not be revealed to her until the bridegroom actually appeared at her door.[30]

As we have accepted what Christ has poured out for us on the cross and signaled our willingness by drinking of the cup He poured for us. The Fellowship that is desired is acknowledged by breaking bread with Him. We now should be maintaining a constant preparedness and watchfulness. And much like the betrothed of Hebrew tradition, we have not been given a date and time for the bridegroom's return and the celebration of the "Marriage Feast". For Jesus replied when asked to give an answer for when:

> *"But of that day and hour knoweth no man, no, not the angels of heaven, but my Father only."*
> *[Matthew 24: 36 KJV]*

This, also, follows the Hebrew custom in that traditionally the bridegroom does not set up a separate dwelling apart from the father but adds rooms to the family home. Only when the Father says that all is ready will the Bridegroom go and fetch the bride to Himself.

---

[30] Smith, haRold. 2015. "Jewish Betrothal Customs." *Hethathasanear.* Accessed 2015. hethathasanear.com/Betrothal.html.

## VII. Worshiping

Worship can be defined as an extravagant respect or admiration for or devotion to one held in esteem. It is the reverence offered to the one so held in love and respect. Worship is the expression of humility in the act of deferring to one greater than self. It is the due offering by the forgiven and accepted to the one who has made it possible. It is the due offering to the one who makes all loving provision for our well-being. It is what is due offering of gratitude and love to the one who gently instructs, chides and comforts us throughout our journeys.

Worship is not something done only by gathering on the Lords day and on certain holy days; but it is to be expressed daily within with our priestly preparations for the day. These are done individually within each of our tents of meeting [our body] when we go to meet with God in study, prayer and obedience. It is communicated by our walking before Him in our daily work and play. Then it is found in our gathering together for instruction and encouragement. Lastly it is in the witness we bring before the world around us when we serve the needs with love and compassion as the emissaries of our Lord.

### Inner Meeting Place:

This is the individual inner space where we withdraw to meet with God the Holy Spirit. It is analogous to the Tent of Meeting given to Moses. It is our personal space where we keep our holy fire burning with our offerings of Sweet Savor. These offerings were a continual and continuous process. First there was the Altar of Incense where the sweet aroma of our love and praise rise before God. Then there are the Lamps of knowledge that comes from being under the tutelage of the Holy Spirit. This begins with study of the loved one to know his character and likes and dislikes, each of us should be able to call to mind readily these things. Lastly there is the Table of His Joy and Provision, where in confidence we share our concerns and are assured of His joy in our trust and love. But this requires that we stand guard over the precincts of that seat within our souls where He has come to reside. For our meeting with God individually requires that we prevent "idols" from encroaching and causing the Spirit to withdraw until the interlopers are dealt with. Then it takes spending time conversing, listening and yielding to the one that is our beloved. Lastly it entails bringing our lives into obedience to His sovereign will, discussing with him our thoughts and plans and then waiting on His timing.

Outward signs of our worship are both the fruits of our cultivation as exhibited in our character as we become more like Him and the works we perform in His Will. We should strive under His help and guidance to cultivate the fruits always conscious that our works and services are the sweet savor offerings we present to Him as expressions of gratitude and love. For we have not obtained our freedom by works but by His Grace, and it only because of this freedom that we are able to commit ourselves to our betrothed.

> "For it is by grace you have been saved, through faith — and this is not from yourselves, it is the gift of God — not by works, so that no one can boast." [Ephesians 2: 8, 9]

A list of the fruits that we should be cultivating as we grow and serve are found in Galatians 5 verses 22 and 23 and are essential to our being Christ's ambassadors to the world. Sometimes it is only when we exhibit the grace of these fruits that the world has a glimpse of our beloved.

> *"But the fruit of the Spirit is <u>love</u>, <u>joy</u>, <u>peace</u>, <u>forbearance</u>, <u>kindness</u>, <u>goodness</u>, <u>faithfulness</u>, <u>gentleness</u>, and <u>self-control</u>. Against such things there is no law."*

It is only when we have the humility that comes with our recognition of our need for what has been offered, then our cultivating the fruits, which no law forbids, are we prepared to be the preserving force that we are meant to be. As we display these things the light of God shines out to the surrounding world. For it is God's desire is that none should die but be preserved for life. In the practice of these thing we create a wonder about what should have produced this result. So as well as being the salt that brings savor and preservation we bring a light to shine on the path to a better way.

It is here where we maintain our altar of incense with the continual fire of our prayers. Sending up the sweet savor offerings of our desire for an intimate relationship with Him. It is the most important of the altar fires for it is from here that the flame is brought out to light the fires on the altars of the churches local and catholic.

## Corporate gathering in the outer Court:

This would be the gathering together that we are counselled to participate in for the strengthening of the brothers and sisters on the Sabbath/Lord's day. For God's purpose for the Church is that we are to be His witnesses to the world. To effectively perform our purpose He knows that we need the support and encouragement of the likeminded to do His will. This in a sense would be our entering into the Altar Court and Court of the Gentiles of the old Temple and Tabernacle complex. This is the place that was designed to give the Christian opportunity for affirmation, instruction and accountability. This is also where we are to bring out our offerings of fire to be joined with other such fires to shine before the world.

> *All the nations gather together and the peoples assemble. Which of their gods foretold this and proclaimed to us the former things? Let them bring in their witnesses to prove they were right, so that others may hear and say, "It is true." "You are my witnesses," declares the Lord, "and my servant whom I have chosen, so that you may know and believe me and understand that I am he. Before me no god was formed, nor will there be one after me."* [Isaiah 43: 9, 10]

We all like the companionship found when we know that there are others travelling with us on this journey. So that our gathering together in His name reassures us that we travel with others of like mind. Then as Proverbs tells us we gain strength and sharpness when we share and exchange our thoughts, ideas and plans.

"As iron sharpens iron, so one person sharpens another." [Proverbs 27: 17]

Then again the writer of Hebrews counsels us that we can and should encourage and lift one another up.

*"And let us consider how we may spur one another on toward love and good deeds, not giving up meeting together, as some are in the habit of doing, but encouraging one another — and all the more as you see the Day approaching." [Hebrews 10: 24, 25]*

So God expects us and wants us to meet together for instruction, encouragement, correction and so that by many voices our witness for Him will gain strength.

An essential function of this gathering together is the one that allows another to better see what one has missed, misunderstood or when one has gone astray. It is within this group that we can expect loving correction when we make missteps in our walk. For when the correction is lovingly made amendment of one's ways can be achieved with greater certainty for not one of us can claim perfect performance and knowledge. So yes we are to help one another as we strive to follow Christ on our individual journeys, we are to carefully consider our words in the light and understanding of God's word as illuminated by the instruction of the Holy Spirit.

*"All Scripture is God-breathed and is useful for teaching, rebuking, correcting and training in righteousness, so that the servant of God may be thoroughly equipped for every good work." [2 Timothy 3: 16, 17]*

When we have people who love us to hold us accountable we are better able to achieve more than we had thought. We gain a confidence that would not come were we without the fellowship of others.

When we are in fellowship, we find that others have talents, strengths and resources that complement ours so that the end results are greater than when done solo. So we are encouraged to seek the assistance of our brethren to perform our acts of offering to God's glory. Jealousy to acquire accolades is discouraged as much as is the envy of another's recognition. Yet as we bring our fires to the main altar of the Church we are cautioned not to bring in doctrines and customs that are not of God but of our own devising or after our own desires for these things will be rejected by God with unforeseen consequences. This is the intent of the warning found in Leviticus 10: 1-3[31] about bringing unauthorized fire to the Lord's altar.

> *"Aaron's sons Nadab and Abihu took their censers, put fire in them and added incense; and they offered unauthorized fire before the Lord, contrary to his command. So fire came out from the presence of the Lord and consumed them, and they died before the Lord. Moses then said to Aaron, "This is what the Lord spoke of when he said: 'Among those who approach me I will be proved holy; in the sight of all the people I will be honored.'"* [Leviticus 10: 1-3]

So in our walk with God we should study to understand His teachings and wait for His leadings as we offer our fires at His altars.

---

[31] Swedenborg, E. 2006. *Spiritual Meanings & Correspondences of Specific Words in the Bible.* Accessed July 15, 2015. http://www.biblemeanings. info/Words/Natural/Strangefire.htm.

Susan E. Craig

## Concord of the body:

Derivation of the word concord comes to us from the Middle English word that means agreeing from the heart.[32] We are enjoined to work for this happy state within the body of Christ. When the entire church humbly and in gentleness demonstrates concord within Christ it becomes a force to be reckoned with in the surrounding arena.

> *"As a prisoner for the Lord, then, I urge you to live a life worthy of the calling you have received. Be completely humble and gentle; be patient, bearing with one another in love. Make every effort to keep the unity of the Spirit through the bond of peace."* [Ephesians 4: 1-3]

This concord is a twofold proposition, in the first instance we need to find concord within the local fellowship and then we need to find concord within the body of Christ at large. This is so that we may present a coherent and cohesive picture of God's loving kindnesses and desires for the world. We must look beyond our differences of style and ritual to find a single heartedness in Christ. Many of our squabbles and discords seem to be around the forms of worship and not the central core of our hope in salvation. This discord gives unbelievers something to hold against the Church in its entirety. As our discord aids in their desire to discount the truth of God and the beauty of following in Christ's steps. The more we model Christ with each other the greater chance we have of attracting those who have yet to know Him.

---

[32] Harper, Douglas. 2015. *Online Etymology Dictionary*. Accessed 2015. http://www.etymonline.com/index.php?term=concord.

The Apostle Paul gave us the following picture of how we are to present ourselves for the world to be able to see Christ in and through us. It is instruction not only for dealing with the world at large but also our brothers and sisters in Christ. It is so out of the ordinary that it will stand out visibly from the surrounding societies. But it behooves us as Christ's ambassadors and God's exemplars before the world to strive to conform to these standards.

> *"Therefore, as God's chosen people, holy and dearly loved, clothe yourselves with compassion kindness, humility, gentleness and patience."* [Colossians 3: 12]

This description is not the natural reactions in human nature and is counterintuitive to common thought. So when those of the world encounter a people who act in this way it has difficulty comprehending or believing this is real. The world, also, has little argument against these things. Here are the definitions of these characteristics we are to cultivate.

- Compassion: sympathetic ability to be awake and understand another's distress together with a desire to alleviate it and willing ability to understand
- Kindness: having a state of having or showing a gentle nature and a desire to help others: wanting and liking to do good things and to bring happiness to others
- Humility: the quality or state of not thinking you are better than other people

- Gentleness: the quality of having or showing a kind and quiet nature: not harsh or violent
- Patience: the capacity, habit, or fact of being able to bear pains or trials calmly or without complaint and manifesting the ability to choose to take the actions of retaliation, one is capable of doing under provocation or strain: not acting hastily but steadfast despite opposition, difficulty, or adversity[33]

We have been warned that division within in the body will destroy the function and purpose of that body. We are called the body of Christ so we should work to set aside the animosities that have arisen out of choices in form and preferences in worship. As with any body, in order to function there will be highly visible parts and those parts not seen by any. But all are necessary and valuable to the proper functioning of the body. Petty bickering, envy and jealousy should have no place in the body, the only undisputable criteria should be, "Christ is Lord and Savior, and He is risen and is at the Right Hand of God" and that the Bible is the true "Word of God", his love letter to us. In this love letter we find guidance, instruction and correction, for it is a complete set of the standards, requirements and offers of restoration to our covenant relationship with God.

*"The Holy Scriptures, which are able to make you wise for salvation through faith in Christ Jesus. All Scripture is God-breathed and is useful for teaching, rebuking, correcting and training in righteousness, so that the servant of God may be thoroughly equipped for every good work."*
*[2 Timothy 3: 15-17]*

---

[33] Webster, Merriam. n.d.

Within this framework there is room for many differing tastes in form, custom, music and exuberance. In Revelation, we find several times the reference that in heaven we will still be distinguishable and individual, as it is recorded that there will be people *"from every nation, tribe, people and language, standing before the throne and before the Lamb"[Revelation 7: 9]*. So while we are called to unity, unity does not imply sameness. Unity carries the idea of uniquenesses joined in a harmony of purpose. If everyone is the same then someone is unnecessary and we have been instructed by God that each of us has a purpose and a value beyond valuation. As such a conformity in sameness of appearance will not be asked of us. But a unity in love and the worship of the LORD is required of us. For Jesus has said:

> *"Jesus knew their thoughts and said to them: "Any kingdom divided against itself will be ruined, and a house divided against itself will fall." [Luke 11: 17]*

We are cautioned to keep our disputes within house. This is because when we make our internal squabbles public we diminish our ability reflect glory to God. As the Apostle Paul counseled the church at Corinth:

> "If any of you has a dispute with another, do you dare to take it before the ungodly for judgment instead of before the Lord's people?" [1 Corinthians 6: 1]

Therefore we should strive not to let our differences and disputes to become public entertainment but to take them before God in prayer. Our single constant concern should be to reflect glory to God as His representatives to the world.

In addition to our desire to reflect glory upon God, it is our ministry to foster reconciliation not only between God and man, but also, to bring peoples of all ranks, stations, cultures and races together in Christ, for it is God's desire that we become one family. Thus if we cannot demonstrate a love and a coming together between our various brothers and sisters, we weaken our ability to facilitate our reconciliation efforts with the world.

> *"All this is from God, who reconciled us to himself through Christ and gave us the ministry of reconciliation: that God was reconciling the world to himself in Christ, not counting people's sins against them. And he has committed to us the message of reconciliation. We are therefore Christ's ambassadors, as though God were making his appeal through us. We implore you on Christ's behalf: Be reconciled to God." [2 Corinthians 5: 18-20]*

If we continue to divide for surface and sometimes superficial causes how can we say we are all one in Christ's eyes and love. For as we serve a Lord who makes no distinction between peoples other than what they do with God's son neither should we.

> *"I now realize how true it is that God does not show favoritism but accepts from every nation the one who fears him and does what is right." [Acts 10: 34-35]*

# CHAPTER 11

*⟨decorative flourish⟩*

## New Covenant Conclusion

Since the Creation, it has been God's desire for us to be with Him in His Kingdom. This was the intent when He created Eden and gave man a purpose under God's sovereignty as stewards and guardians of Eden in close association with Him. We, man, rebelled and suffered the consequence of being exiled from our home (Eden) to become sojourners in a far place. Since that time God has indicated over and over again His purposes for man remains the same. But in order for that to happen, a return to our first love and purpose is required. Throughout Bible history, God has given us instructions and patterns to learn from.

In the case of our current Ingathering Journey, we can look to Israel's sojourn in Egypt. They went there and at first were respected and accepted. But gradually became enslaved to the world they found themselves in. They found themselves in much the condition that is familiar today. Trapped in their situation prisoners of a cruel tyrant, with a promise that was inaccessibly out of reach. Then God provided a way. He then led them on a long journey of testing and trial before bringing them into the land of promise.[34] Along the way as trials of the unknown arose the people looked back to the times that were familiar even though uncomfortable or damaging.

In the fulfillment of God's promises for the first Advent of the Messiah, we have reassurance for our confidence in the many promises in both the Old and New Testament of the Messiah's returning to gather His people into His Kingdom once more and then to rule and reign. It has been said that throughout Scripture there are at least three times more references to His coming in the Day of the Lord than there were to the first Advent. With this confidence and hope, we again have a tent of meeting where God offers to travel with us. This Tabernacle, like the original, should be tended by a priest keeping before God the daily offerings requested and guarded from the "strange fires" of our own desires, wishes and misinterpretations of His Word.

So on our walk with God as He prepares to gather us again to Him there is much that the first ingathering can tell us of how we should proceed. The quiet time spent in our Tabernacle seeking His counsel prepares us to perform our priestly function. The teaching and love shared during this time increases our ability and desire to know and be known as fit partners for Him as His beloved betrothed. In meeting regularly with our Sovereign to understand His desires, plans and timing suits us to perform our ambassadorial function to the world who does not know Him. The more we come to know and admire His ways, the more the world will be able to see Him for when they see us they see Him in us.

Individually, we each have a Tent of Meeting where we can repair for comfort, guidance and counsel. In fact we are

---

[34] Goldsworthy, Graeme; MA, ThD. 1981. "Gospel and Kingdom, A Christian Interpretation of the Old Testament." In *Gospel and Kingdom, A Christian Interpretation of the Old Testament*, by Graeme Goldsworthy, 44-62. Exeter: Paternoster Press.

instructed to do so and so to seek His face. This tent is first to be covered just as the one of old with the fourfold coverings provided by the work of Christ. He has covered us in His righteousness. He has covered our debts of sin with His sacrifice. He has been our substitutionary restitution for our transgressions. Lastly, He has offered us the protection of His sheltering arms. So once we have accepted His covering we are permitted to receive into our tents the honor and glory of the Holy Spirit. As we grow in the Holy Spirit's comfort, instruction and guidance the more we become like unto Christ and fully accredited ambassadors of the glory of God. Thus bringing joy to Abba, Father's heart.

We have been tasked with tending and guarding our Tabernacles. Keeping it free from idolatry so that when we seek Him in our Holy of Holies, He will not have withdrawn. As He is holy, He will withdraw from places that are polluted or have not been attended to for some time. This means we are to maintain the Inner Court of our tent keeping it continuously supplied with the light from His Word, remembering with thanksgiving His presence in our lives, His provision for our daily needs, and rejoicing in the depth of His love. Here in our Inner Court we bring especially our offerings that are the sweet aroma of our praises and love. It is here that we prepare carefully our fire in His will and instruction. This is so that we bring to the public altar a pure and accepted fire. This to demonstrate before all the world who God is and we are his emissaries to those around us.

Corporately we are not to forsake the gathering together in worship, instruction, fellowship, comfort and encouragement. It is in this body that the work of the Lord is brought forward and implemented. It is there where we reach out to our brothers and sisters in Christ locally and around the world. This is the Outer Court where the world can come to learn of God and to be welcomed by God's ambassadors. It is there where our example of caring for one another gives substance to our professions of belief, faith and love. As our citizenship is in Heaven our physical churches should be Heaven's Embassies to the surrounding community serving not only our fellow citizens but facilitating enquiries and instruction of those wishing to obtain to this citizenship.

For now that we are privileged walk daily with God as His children, the Holy Spirit has come into our tent. He has come to be our Wonderful Counselor that Isaiah promised. He is the one we can repair to in times of turmoil and fear as He is our Comforter and has come alongside to bear us up on our journey. We can stumble and rise for He has promised to be our Advocate and Intercessor before the Judgement Seat.

Because we have answered His call and accepted positions as priests in the Royal Priesthood of the Messiah Jesus Christ we are to walk before Him as His ambassadors the visible representations of Him to a fallen world. We have the privilege of standing in the gap for the unsaved, interceding for them and showing the way to those willing to see and hear. This is what serving in and for His Church means.

We will bring joy and a sweet aroma offering to our betrothed, to our loving God, when as the Psalmist wrote we can sing:

*"Your statutes are wonderful;*
*Therefore I obey them.*
*The unfolding of your words gives light;*
*It gives understanding to the simple.*
*I open my mouth and pant,*
*Longing for your commands.*

*Turn to me and have mercy on me,*
*As you always do to those who love your name.*
*Direct my footsteps according to your word;*
*Let no sin rule over me.*
*Redeem me from human oppression,*
*That I may obey your precepts.*
*Make your face shine on your servant*
*And teach me your decrees."*
*[Psalm 119: 129-135]*

# POSTLUDE

## Come Tabernacle with God
### A Song of Return

Within me a great joy arose
For Abba has called to me "Come home"
For His Love my heart yearns
His reassurance comforts and strengthens me
For while on my travel home
There will be hazards
Stumbling blocks will litter my way
But I shall not be dissuaded
For Abba calls and wants me to come
Abba sent His Love to find me
He yearns for His children
He has provided for us a guide
One who has gone before and informs our way
He has created a refuge for me
A shelter when the tempests overwhelm
He sent one to redeem me
And set me free for the return

He gave me a Comforter
To counsel, to guide and encourage
Yes, One to walk on the road with me
A companion along the way
So I will enter His tent with singing
Calling to others to join in the journey
For I will journey secure in His Tabernacle.

S.E.C.

# FOOTNOTES

## Introduction

Pg. xviii – [1] Moses (Genesis 12: 7 and Genesis 15: 14). 1973. *Holy Bible.* Grand Rapids, Michigan: Zondervan. Accessed 2015.

Pg. xxii – [2] 2000 - 2014. *Abarim Publications: sources.* http://www.abarim-publications.com/Meaning/Israel.html#.VVaRIPlViko

## The Community of God at Creation

Pg. 4 – [3] Beale, G. K. 2004. *The Temple and the Church's Mission; a biblical theology of the dwelling place of God.* Downers Grove, Illinois: Intervarsity Press

## Covenants

Pg. 18 – [4] Benner, Jeff A. 2004. *The Holy Assembly and the Everlasting Covenant.* Accessed 2015. http://www.ancient-hebrew.org/ holyassembly/chapter1.html.

Pg. 19 – [5] Hamilton, Jeffrey W. 2013. *The Importance of Covenants - Part II.* Accessed May 19, 2015. http://www.lavistachurchofchrist.org/LVSermons/ImportanceOfCovenants2.html.

Pg. 19 – [6] Farlex. 2015. *The Free Dictionary Legal.* Accessed May 16, 2015. http://legal-ictionary.thefreedictionary.com/assigns

Pg. 29 – [7] Grisanti, Michael A. 1999. *The Davidic Covenant.* 10 2. Accessed May 20, 2015. The Davidic Covenant TMS.pdf.

**Prophets**

Pg. 31 – [8] Henry, Matthew. N.d. *Matthew Henry Commentary on the Whole Bible, various prophets.*

Pg. 32 – [9] 2000 - 2014. *Abarim Publications: sources* http://www.abarim-publications.com/Meaning/Hosea.html# .VaQIDvlViko

Pg. 32 – [10] 2000 - 2014. *Abarim Publications: sources* http://www.abarim-publications.com/Meaning/Gomer.html #.VaQKovlVikp

Pg. 33 – [11] 2000 - 2014. *Abarim Publications: sources* http://www.abarim-publications.com/Meaning/Beeri.html# .Vj4EaLerRG8

Pg. 45 – [12] Dolphin, Lambert. 2013. *The Destruction of the Second Temple.* June 27. Accessed May 2015. http://www.templemount.org/destruct2.html

Pg. 45 – [13] Times, Messianic. 2014. *Tisha B'Av Israel and the Horrible, No Good, Very Bad Day.* 8 1. Accessed 5 23, 2015. http://www.mjaa.gorg/site/News2?id=9086&security=1.

Pg. 45 – [14] 2000 - 2014. *Abarim Publications: sources.* http://www.abarim-publications.com/Meaning/Haggai.html #.VUQu4PlViko.

## Commandments, Law & Custom

Pg. 54 – [15] Chan, Amanda L. 2014. *8 Ways Forgiveness Is Good For Your Health.* 10 26. Accessed 5 20, 2015. http://www. huffingtonpost.com/2014/10/25/forgiveness-health-benefits_n_6029736.html

Pg. 65 – [16] Wheeler, John. 2015. *Music of the Bible Revealed.* June 25. Accessed July 9, 2015. http://www.rakkav.com/ biblemusic/pages/suzanne.htm.

## Festival of Tabernacles

Pg. 74 – [17] Parsons, John J. 2003. *The Festival of Sukkot - the Feast of Tabernacles.* Accessed June 2, 2015. http://www. hebrew4christians.com/Holidays/Fall_Holidays/ Sukkot/sukkot.html.

## Old Testament Temple/Tabernacle

Pg. 80 – [18] n.d. *Covering of the Sanctuary.* Accessed April 2015. http://www.templebuildersministry.com/Index_ Tabernacle_of_Moses_6.php.

Pg. 82 – [19] Cohen, Peter. 2012. *Messianic Good News.* October 4. Accessed May 1, 2015. http://www.messianicgoodnews. org/part-4-the-bread-of-the-presence/.

Pg. 89 - [20] Beale, G. K. 2004. *The Temple and the Church's Mission; a biblical theology of the dwelling place of God.* Downers Grove, Illinois: Intervarsity Press.

## Priesthood

Pg. 100 – [21] 1906. *SHOWBREAD*. Accessed May 2015. http://jewishencyclopedia.com/articles/13611-showbread.

Pg. 108 – [22] n.d. *Temple Institute The Priestly Garments*

## Sacrifices and Offerings under the Mosaic Covenant

Pg. 115 – [23] Mamre, Mechon. 2012. *Qorbanot: Sacrifices and Offerings*. January 24. Accessed May 5, 2015. http://www.mechon-mamre.org/jewfaq/qorbanot.htm.

Pg. 116 – [24] 2015. *The Five Levitical Offerings*. Accessed 2015. http://www.bible-history.com/TAB4The_5_Levitical_Offerings.htm.

Pg. 122 – [25] Langham, Andrew. 2006. "biblecentre.org/." "Topics/al_drink_offering.htm. Dec Friday 22.

## Sacrifices and Offerings under the New Covenant

Pg. 125 – [26] Orville Boyd Jenkins, Ed.D., Ph.D. 2007. *Reflections Debts or Tresspasses*. November 22.

Pg. 127 – [27] Elwell, Walter A. 1997. *Offerings and Sacrifices*. Accessed May 1, 2015. http://www.biblestudytools.com/dictionaries/bakers-evangelical-dictionary/offerings-and-sacrifices.html.

## Feasts & Festivals

Pg. 128 – [28] n.d. *Orah Sheb Yshua.*

Pg. 131 – [29] n.d. *Biblestudytools.org.* bakers evangelical dictionary feasts and festivals of israel

## Obligations

Pg. 151 – [30] Smith, haRold. 2015. "Jewish Betrothal Customs." *Hethathasanear.* Accessed 2015. hethathasanear.com/ Betrothal.html.

Pg. 157 – [31] Swedenborg, E. 2006. *Spiritual Meanings & Correspondences of Specific Words in the Bible.* Accessed July 15, 2015. http://www.biblemeanings.info/Words/ Natural/Strangefire.htm.

Pg. 158 – [32] Harper, Douglas. 2015. *Online Etymology Dictionary.* Accessed 2015. http://www.etymonline.com/ index.php?term=concord

Pg. 160 – [33] Webster, Merriam. n.d.

## Conclusion

Pg. 164 - [34] Goldsworthy, Graeme; MA, ThD. 1981. "Gospel and Kingdom, A Christian Interpretation of the Old Testament. By Graeme Goldsworthy, 44-62. Exeter: Paternoster Press.

# BIBLIOGRAPHY

Moses (Genesis 12: 7 and Genesis 15: 14). 1973. *Holy Bible.* Grand Rapids, Michigan: Zondervan. Accessed 2015.

2000 - 2014. *Abarim Publications: sources.* Accessed 2015. http://www.abarim-publications.com/Meaning/ Haggai.html#.VUQu4PlViko.

Beale, G. K. 2004. *The Temple and the Church's Mission; a biblical theology of the dwelling place of God.* Downers Grove, Illinois: Intervarsity Press.

Benner, Jeff A. 2004. *The Holy Assembly and the Everlasting Covenant.* Accessed 2015. http://www.ancient-hebrew. org/holyassembly/chapter1.html.

n.d. *Bible Gateway.* Accessed 2015. https://www. biblegateway.com/.

n.d. *Biblestudytools.org.* http://www.biblestudytools.com/ dictionaries/bakers-evangelical-dictionary/feasts-and-festivals-of-israel.html.

Chan, Amanda L. 2014. *8 Ways Forgiveness Is Good For Your Health.* 10 26. Accessed 5 20, 2015. http://www.

huffingtonpost.com/2014/10/25/forgiveness-health-benefits_n_6029736.html.

Cohen, Peter. 2012. *Messianic Good News.* October 4. Accessed May 1, 2015. http://www.messianicgoodnews.org/part-4-the-bread-of-the-presence/.

n.d. *Covering of the Sanctuary.* Accessed April 2015. http://www.templebuildersministry.com/Index_Tabernacle_of_Moses_6.php.

Dolphin, Lambert. 2013. *The Destruction of the Second Temple.* June 27. Accessed May 2015. http://www.templemount.org/destruct2.html.

Elwell, Walter A. 1997. *Offerings and Sacrifices.* Accessed May 1, 2015. http://www.biblestudytools.com/dictionaries/bakers-evangelical-dictionary/offerings-and-sacrifices.html.

Farlex. 2015. *The Free Dictionary Legal.* Accessed May 16, 2015. http://legal-dictionary.thefreedictionary.com/assigns.

Graeme Goldsworthy, MA, ThD. 1981. "Gospel and Kingdom, A Christian Interpretation of the Old Testament." In *Gospel and Kingdom, A Christian Interpretation of the Old Testament,* by Graeme Goldsworthy, 44-62. Exeter: Paternoster Press.

Grisanti, Michael A. 1999. *The Davidic Covenant.* 10 2. Accessed May 20, 2015. The Davidic Covenant TMS.pdf.

Hamilton, Jeffrey W. 2013. *The Importance of Covenants - Part II*. Accessed May 19, 2015. http://www.lavistachurchofchrist. org/LVSermons/ImportanceOfCovenants2.html.

Harper, Douglas. 2015. *Online Etymology Dictionary*. Accessed 2015. http://www.etymonline.com/index. php?term=concord.

Henry, Matthew. n.d. *Matthew Henry Commentary on the Whole Bible*. Accessed April 2015. http://www.biblestudytools. com/commentaries/matthew-henry-complete/.

Langham, Andrew. 2006 . "biblecentre.org/." *topics/ al_drink_offering.htm*. Dec Friday 22. Accessed April April 13, 14 2015, 2015. http://www.biblecentre.org/ topics/al_drink_offering.htm.

Mamre, Mechon. 2012. *Qorbanot: Sacrifices and Offerings*. January 24. Accessed May 5, 2015. http://www.mechon-mamre.org/jewfaq/qorbanot.htm.

n.d. *Orah Sheb Yshua*. http://osyministries.com/index. php?option=com_content&view=article&id=161:the-biblical-feasts-chart&catid=44:osy-study-docs.

Orville Boyd Jenkins, Ed.D., Ph.D. 2007. *Reflections Debts or Tresspasses*. November 22. Accessed April 2015. http:// orvillejenkins.com/jenkins/reflections/debts.html.

Parsons, John J. 2003. *The Festival of Sukkot - the Feast of Tabernacles*. Accessed June 2, 2015. http://www. hebrew4christians.com/Holidays/Fall_Holidays/ Sukkot/sukkot.html.

Roberts, Rev. Dr. Mark D. 2011. *Introduction to the Christian Year.* Accessed May 9, 2015. http://www.patheos.com/blogs/markdroberts/series/introduction-to-the-christian-year/.

1906. *SHOWBREAD.* Accessed May 2015. http://jewishencyclopedia.com/articles/13611-showbread.

Smith, haRold. 2015. "Jewish Betrothal Customs." *Hethathasanear.* Accessed 2015. hethathasanear.com/Betrothal.html.

Swedenborg, E. 2006. *Spiritual Meanings & Correspondences of Specific Words in the Bible.* Accessed July 15, 2015. http://www.biblemeanings.info/Words/Natural/Strangefire.htm.

n.d. *Temple Institute The Priestly Garments.* http://www.templeinstitute.org/priestly_garments.htm.

2015. *The Five Levitical Offerings.* Accessed 2015. http://www.bible-history.com/tabernacle/TAB4The_5_Levitical_Offerings.htm.

Times, Messianic. 2014. *Tisha B'Av Israel and the Horrible, No Good, Very Bad Day .* 8 1. Accessed 5 23, 2015. http://www.mjaa.org/site/News2?id=9086&security=1.

Webster, Merriam. n.d. *http://www.merriam-webster.com/dictionary/compassion.*

Wheeler, John. 2015. *Music of the Bible Revealed.* June 25. Accessed July 9, 2015. http://www.rakkav.com/biblemusic/pages/suzanne.htm.

Printed in the United States
By Bookmasters